The Essentials of Surfing

The authoritative guide to waves, equipment, etiquette, safety, and instructions for surfriding

KEVIN D. LAFFERTY

Copyright © 2013 Kevin D. Lafferty

Illustrations Copyright © 2013 JR Johnson

Cover Design by JR Johnson

All rights reserved.

Overhead Press

Santa Barbara, California

ISBN-13: 978-0-9912088-0-7

CONTENTS

1	So You Want To Learn To Surf?	1
2	Waves	5
3	Surfboards	17
4	Board Care	27
5	What To Wear	33
6	Etiquette	41
7	Safety	47
8	Getting Ready	63
9	Your First Session	75
10	Beyond Beginning	93
11	Now Go Surfing	99
	About the Author	100
	Glossary	101

PROLOGUE

The Essentials of Surfing is a textbook for surfing and an owner's manual for a surfboard. You can't learn to surf by reading a book, but *The Essentials of Surfing* will give you the knowledge you need to be more confident about learning to surf, avoid conflicts with other surfers, and diminish your chances of becoming a productive member of society.

The Essentials of Surfing has useful information for surfers of all levels, but it does not cover advanced topics, like pulling aerials, conquering big waves, or tube riding, nor does it teach other sports like bodysurfing, kitesurfing, or carsurfing.

The Essentials of Surfing starts out by describing waves, the main resource of surfing. It then lists the many types of surfboards you will see in the water, explaining which ones work best for learning and how to care for your own board. You'll also get advice on what to wear in the water to protect you from sun, rashes, and the cold. Most importantly, *The Essentials of Surfing* lists the informal rules of surfing to help you get along with other surfers in the line up. Surfing is not as dangerous as driving to the beach, but *The Essentials of Surfing* outlines common hazards and how you can protect yourself from them. If this doesn't put you off, you can read a step-by-step lesson in surfing your first wave. *The Essentials of Surfing* then gives general advice on how to advance beyond the beginner level. A glossary at the end lists some technical jargon and slang specific to surfing. Read straight through to get the big picture. Then, use it as a reference as you learn. When you're done, teach a friend and give it to them.

After reading *The Essentials of Surfing*, you will be informed about the realities of surfing. Maybe you'll decide to take up surfing, or perhaps you'll realize it's not for you. If surfing is for you, you'll be able to converse with other surfers and know what to look in a surf shop. When you leave the shop and head to the beach, you'll be able to better understand the waves and what surfers are doing on them. This will help you learn faster and smarter.

1. SO YOU WANT TO LEARN TO SURF?

"I can't surf…..And neither can you."
--*I Can't Surf* (Heath/Wallace/Bentley), Reverend Horton Heat, 1994

The blond dropped into a big wave but couldn't set the rail of his board. The board spiraled away as his body pitched forward. With a crunch, the wave buried him. The next wave peaked, and another surfer took three strokes to push his *Lightning Bolt* pintail down the face, disappearing behind the falling lip. The heaving barrel collapsed and exhaled a blast of spray, out of which Gerry Lopez glided, his arms at his sides, shoulders slouched, as if waiting for a bus. Once the crowd on the beach caught their breath, they cheered. I was a kid viewing the 1972 Pipeline Masters surf contest on ABC-TV's *Wide World of Sports*. I'd just seen my first surfing, and it made me want to learn to surf.

Back then, beginners like me learned slowly by mimicking other surfers. There were no books, no lessons, and no Internet forecasts. Being in the dark about what to do often led to failure. I would have suffered less and surfed better had I known then what I know now. Like any other aging surfer, I've learned a bit over the years. In fact, there is so much to surfing that I thought it needed its own textbook. *The Essentials of Surfing* passes on my four decades of surfing experience to make it easier for you to learn to surf than it was for me.

Why Surf?

There's no doubt catching a wave is an adrenaline rush, but it is also a brief, wet, spiritual experience. Surfer Bill Hamilton said "Surfing equates to living in the very moment of 'now'." Likewise, when the Beach Boys sang "Catch a wave and you're sitting on top of the world", they were describing a joyful experience in which your everyday troubles and stresses disappear. "This man had the most supreme pleasure while he was driven so fast and so smoothly by the sea." British explorer Captain James Cook (1728-1779) remarked when he first watched a surfer in Hawaii. Surfers will even tell you that surfing saved their lives or inspired them to be better people. It sounds hokey, but surfers are less depressed and anxious; they enjoy nature; they are not as concerned with the outside world, and have a heightened focus about their lives. When I catch a wave, time slows; my thoughts blur, then I paddle out to do it again. Adrenaline rush or spiritual experience, catch one wave and you'll want another. It's like crack cocaine, but wetter.

Much of the allure of surfing has to do with being in the ocean and harnessing the energy of the waves and nature. How good can that be? When asked what he would do if he had one free day, U.S. President Barack Obama did not say that he would like to clear brush on his ranch, or play a round of golf with a senator, or hook up with an intern, he said:

"…You jump in the ocean. And you have to wait until there is a break in the waves. . . . and if you catch the right wave you cut left because left is west. . . . Then you cut down into the tube there. You might see the crest rolling and you might see the sun glittering. You might see a sea turtle in profile, sideways, like a hieroglyph in the water. . . . And you spend an hour out there. And if you've had a good day you've caught six or seven good waves and six or seven not so good waves. And you go back to your car. With a soda or a can of juice. And you sit. And you can watch the sun go down …" (Michael Lewis, Vanity Fair 2012).

You don't have to be POTUS to enjoy the waves. Improvements in equipment and weather forecasting make it far easier to learn to surf than when Captain Cook first saw Hawaiians engaging in the sport of kings. Gone are the hardships for young groms forced to guess when the next batch of waves might arrive, dragging a ninety-pound redwood board to the beach and wearing a wool sweater to beat back the cold. Light, well-engineered surfboards, warm flexible wetsuits, and advances in weather forecasting take a lot of the guesswork out of learning to surf. There's never been an easier time in history to learn to surf.

Despite increased access to the sport, surfing still has a much slower learning curve than other balance sports like snowboarding, skateboarding, or water skiing. Many beginners struggle to stand up and surf straight to the beach on their first day, and it can take years to master surfing. If you just want to have some fun during a beach holiday, get a bodyboard, and you will be riding waves in no time.

In contrast, there is a lot to learn before you can surf well. I see a lot of clueless learners. Like them, you can jump in the water and paddle around without knowing what you are doing, and you'll probably exhaust yourself, drink some seawater, and catch no waves. Or worse, you'll get in the way of other surfers, or hurt yourself, or hurt someone else. Reading *The Essentials of Surfing* will help keep you from being a liability in the water.

As you learn, you'll enter a network of established surfers who will expect you to know the basic but sometimes subtle rules of surfing. If you look or act silly or inexperienced, you won't earn their respect. They might even ask you to get out of the water. And this won't be an invite to party on the beach.

A Note For the Ladies
When I started surfing, I would go months without seeing a female surfer. There were some, and they were chargers, but mostly the girlfriends were on the beach while their boyfriends were in the water. Now, women and girls are regulars at most spots. This is a good thing for women and for surfing. The best surfing style is smooth and graceful, attributes that come naturally to many women. Everything in *The Essentials of Surfing* applies equally to males and females, except the sentence about getting wax in your chest hair.

KEVIN D. LAFFERTY

2. WAVES

**It mounts at sea, a concave wall
Down-ribbed with shine,
And pushes forward, building tall
Its steep incline.**

--*The Wave*, Thom Gunn (2009)

Wind blows the surface of the sea into swells that develop a characteristic height and period as they approach the coast. Here, variation in the seafloor and coastline leads to different types of breaking waves. The tide and wind further groom or ruin these waves for surfers. Although a lot of factors go into making good surfing waves, you don't have to be an oceanographer to have a high wave IQ. Just the basics will do.

Like the Inuit language has a dozen words for snow, surfers have a rich terminology for waves that is not always easy for an outsider to understand. On a good day, surfers will laud the waves as spitting, barreling, or peeling. On a bad day, you'll hear epithets like closed out, mushy, or blown out. Either way, surfers talk more about waves than is considered polite in mixed (non-surfer) company. To talk about waves with a surfer, you'll need to know the surf terms in the Glossary.

What Makes a Swell?

Almost all surfable waves come from wind. As wind blows over water, it creates friction with the surface. The friction converts the wind energy into wave energy that starts as a ripple. As the ripple increases in size, its back acts like a sail that the wind blows forward. While wind blows, ripples grow into bigger and bigger swells that increase in size with wind speed. A 40-knot gale can throw up a 15-foot swell after blowing over 100 miles of ocean. The longer the fetch, or distance over which the wind blows, the larger the swells will be. Swells greater than 20 feet will develop if the same gale blows over a 200-mile fetch, and they can travel a thousand miles away. This is why a storm that destroys someone's house can lead to someone else's barrel. Or, as in one surfer says to another in the film *Sharknado*, "It's a Mexican hurricane. Bad for them, good for us!" (The Asylum, 2013).

Here's some physics that might help you understand how waves work. Open ocean swells move energy forward, but the water particles only travel in a circle, like a Ferris wheel. The circular path of the water molecules decreases in diameter with depth and increases in diameter with the size of the swell.

The time it takes two consecutive swell crests to pass the same point is the swell period (or interval). The period is only four to eight seconds in a windy storm. As a result, the swells are disorganized and choppy, with peaks popping up all over. As the storm abates, the swells keep traveling away from the storm. The choppy bits either combine into longer, more organized swells with 10 to 15-second periods, or they dissipate as they lose energy due to friction with the air. If the swell is far from land, it decays in size once the wind dies, in part because the energy spreads out from the original source in an arc of increasing length. Over time and distance, the swell sorts itself out, and the longer period swells (16-25 seconds) move fast and far. These long-period forerunners will be the first to reach a beach, even wrapping into protected coves. A well-organized, long-period groundswell looks like corduroy. When surfers see a lined-up swell stretching to the horizon, pandemonium can break out. Larger, shorter period waves follow, increasing the consistency of the surf. The swell eventually fades, and surfers go back to school or work.

When a swell approaches land, the base of the swell feels the bottom. This compresses the swell, making it taller. Then, as the swell reaches even shallower water, friction from the bottom slows the swell at its base. But there is much less friction at the crest of the wave, which speeds forward, causing the wave to break. The breaking wave mixes air and liquid in a turbulent mound of whitewater that pushes water molecules toward the beach.

The higher the swell, the bigger the breaking waves will be. Larger waves break in deeper water because they feel the bottom sooner than do smaller waves. On a shallow-sloping beach, the depth of water under a breaking wave is 1.3 times the face height of the wave. In other words, a ten-foot wave breaks in 13 feet of water, whereas a two-foot wave breaks in 2.6 feet of water. If the beach is steep, the waves break in shallower water.

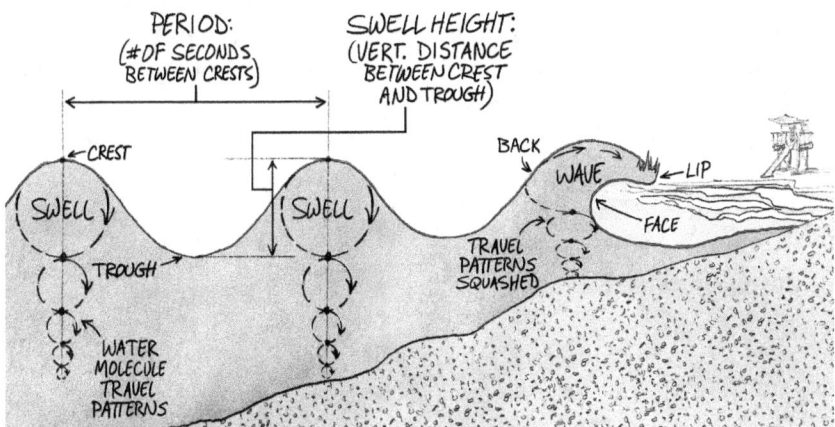

Cross section of breaking waves

Less obvious is that the size of a breaking wave also increases with the period of the swell. Longer-period waves move faster and have more energy. This extra energy leads to higher wave faces when the swell feels the bottom near shore. Although that sounds great, longer period swells lead to less frequent waves. For example, a five-foot swell with a ten-second period might lead to consistent, but disorganized shoulder-high waves, whereas a five-foot swell with a 20-second period might lead to occasional sets of waves that are a few feet overhead. Therefore, knowing the height of the swell is not enough. The period is an equal part of the equation.

The source of a swell determines which surf spots will get waves and which ones will be flat. When weather forecasters indicate a swell direction (west, south, etc.), they refer where the swell is coming from. Swell direction is often measured in degrees where 90° is from the east, 180° is from the south, 270° is from the west and 0/360° is from the north. Each surf break will have a swell "window" from which it can receive waves. For instance, at Rincon Point in Santa Barbara, California, the narrow swell window between 250° and 290° is due to the south-facing coastline and offshore islands that block southern swells. This means that Rincon breaks best during westerly winter swells.

Once a swell hits the coast, the slope of the shoreline affects the power of the breaking waves. If the near-shore area has a gentle sloping bottom, the swell will experience drag for a long distance (called shoaling), and this will decrease the size of the waves and how intense they break, making them ideal for learning. Good breaks for beginners have about one foot of rise per 100 feet of distance (1:100). Most surf breaks have intermediate plunging waves, with a bottom slope averaging 1:30. Steeper bottoms cause waves to surge as they hit the beach. Surging waves are better for body boarders and body surfers than they are for surfers. Variation in bottom slope helps explains why the power of the surf can differ so much from one part of the coast to the other.

The underwater landscape affects where the waves will break. For instance, offshore canyons can focus swell energy onto a beach, leading to larger and more explosive waves there. Submerged canyons in California focus powerful waves at spots like Black's Beach, Point Mugu, and Moss Landing. More commonly, reefs and sandbars will cause waves to break offshore of the beach. This explains why surfers sometimes sit packed together in one part of the surf zone. It's not because we like each other's company.

The shape of the coastline determines how waves break. The waves are more likely to break all at once, in what surfers call a "close out", along a straight coastline. A more complex coastline can create waves with peaks and sloping shoulders. Most breaking waves are in between, with surfable faces punctuated by closeouts. You can sometimes guess where the best waves will be just by looking at a map of the shoreline.

How Big is That Wave?

Although swells are measured from trough to peak, surfers describe the size of breaking waves in a variety of ways. Californians measure the height of a breaking wave from the flat water in front of the wave to the top of the crest (or peak). Hawaiians measure breaking waves in feet from the crest to the following trough (in other words, by looking at the back of the wave from the ocean). A head-high wave in Hawaii is reported as being 2-3', whereas in California, it is 4-6'. In more reasonable parts of the world, they use the metric system, and wave faces are given in meters.

Due to these discrepancies in measurement, I prefer to express the height of a wave face in comparison to an average-sized surfer. Therefore, there are knee-high, waist-high, chest-high, shoulder-high, head-high, overhead, and double-overhead faces. This measure connects wave height to the surfer's experience and is, therefore, least subject to confusion, except if Andre the Giant is describing a wave to Danny DeVito.

Four Types of Breaks
Beach Breaks

Chances are that you will learn to surf at a beach break. Sandy beaches tend to have more amenities for beach goers, and surfing over sand is safer than surfing over rocks. Plus, if the slope of the bottom is shallow, the waves can be mellow and easy to learn on. On a flat sandy bottom, the precise spot that waves break can be difficult to predict. Though this might sound frustrating, unpredictable waves can be good for beginners because there is not a single best peak for good surfers to monopolize. Just sit and wait for a wave to come to you, like a washed car waits for a bird to fly overhead.

A complex bottom helps out a beach break. Sand bars create a focus for waves to break in deeper water, mimicking a reef break. River mouths can also improve beach breaks. They deposit sand bars and their erosive force can carve channels that leave contours along the bottom for waves to break over, sometimes leading to excellent point-break like surf. But sand bottoms shift with the tide and currents, so one session can have breaks different from another.

Classic beach breaks occur along the New Jersey shore, most Brazilian surf spots are beach breaks, and southern California is famous for its beach breaks. The best beach breaks for surfing have intermediate slopes that lead to plunging waves and the occasional barrel. If the bottom is steep, the waves will break top to bottom in shallow water. Such waves are better for body surfing, bodyboarding, or for expert surfers. A good example is Sandy Beach in Oahu where the shore break drops bodysurfers and bodyboarders into a few inches of water. Only a few locals have figured out how to catch these waves with a surfboard. At a heavy break like Sandy Beach, you are more likely to get an earful of sand than catch a wave.

Reef Breaks
Reef breaks occur where rock or coral rises out of deeper water. A reef pass is a special type of reef break that forms in the gap between a fringing coral reef and the lagoon of a tropical island. Swells coming from deep water strike the reef pass, jack up over the shallow coral and then peel in a hollow tube into the mouth of the lagoon. The best waves in French Polynesia are reef passes like Teahupo'o.

 In the surf mags and videos, if you see a perfect barrel of crystal clear water, chances are it was filmed at a coral reef. These are my favorite breaks. But I have a few scars to remind myself that the bottom is shallow and often sharp. The nearness of injury never leaves my mind when the corals below are in sight. Another reason reef breaks are not the best type of wave to learn on is that experienced surfers dominate the best takeoff spots. You might put a trip to a coral reef pass on your bucket list, but wait to get a lot of experience first, or it could kick your bucket.

Still, some reef breaks are excellent places to learn. Waikiki in Oahu, for instance, has a series of gradual sloping reef breaks, many of which produce gentle breaking waves suitable for learning. You won't find a place with more beginning surfers, sunburned Midwesterners, or snorkeling Japanese newlyweds than the reef breaks of Waikiki.

THE ESSENTIALS OF SURFING

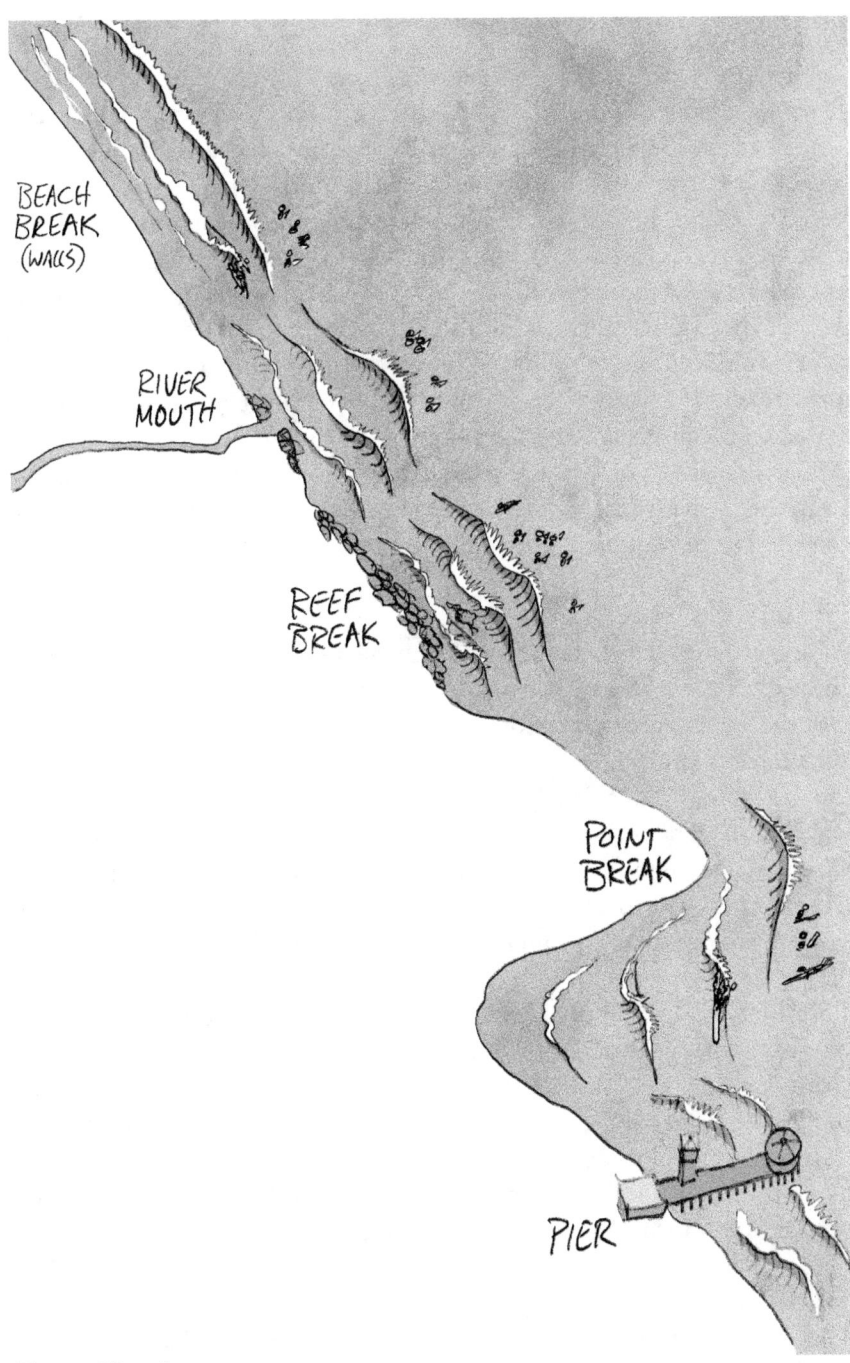

Types of Breaks

Point Breaks

Point breaks can occur at headlands, sand spits, river mouths, or sharp bends in the coastline. A variety of bottom types can form point breaks. Superbank has a sandy bottom, Rincon has a cobble bottom, Jeffrey's Bay has a rocky bench, and Punta de Lobos, and Bells Beach are high rocky headlands jutting out from a sandy bay. At a point break, swells approach the shoreline at an angle and this prevents the wave from breaking all at once. Instead, the breaking part of the wave travels along the shore, leading to rides that can be over a hundred meters long. Like reef breaks, there are one or a few ideal take off spots where crowds focus. Although crowded point breaks can be challenging places for a beginner to get a wave, long predictable rides are great for practicing balance and turning. Malibu Lagoon State Beach is a classic example of a point break that gets crowded with beginners, including the occasional Hollywood A-lister.

Piers, Jetties, Etc.

Along urbanized beaches, it is common to have piers, breakwaters, and jetties. Breakwaters and jetties are built to stabilize harbor mouths or to protect sandy coastlines from eroding. Often, sand accumulates on the up-current side of the structure and erodes from the down current side. These structures can destroy good surfing waves and can be hazardous due to rock, metal, fishing gear, and wood, so be alert for submerged objects if you surf near structures. But, sometimes, structures add variety to an otherwise monotonous bottom topography, forming waves good for surfing.

The Wedge, in Newport Harbor, California, is a freak wave produced by a long jetty at the mouth of Newport Bay. Here, large south swells steered by an offshore canyon reflect off the jetty wall back onto themselves, creating a massive A-frame peak that breaks in shallow water. It's scary enough to body surf the Wedge, let alone try to surf it. At the nearby Huntington Beach Pier, the pilings alter the flow of sand, leading to peaks and channels popular for surf contests.

Tides

The tide can alter the depth of water over bottom features. Most breaks seem to work best on a medium tide. But there are many spots that only work on a high tide and others that only work on a low tide. The best tide for surfing will depend on how the slope of the beach changes with depth. At popular surf spots, the effect of tide is well known by the locals. Don't be shy to ask them.

The easiest thing to predict about the ocean, apart from it being deep, wet, and salty, is the tide. Tides are long-period waves caused by the gravitational pull of the moon with a little help from the sun. The moon pulls the surface of the ocean up toward it. On the side of the earth opposite the moon, there is another, slightly smaller, bulge. If the sun is in line with the moon (i.e., new moon or full moon), this creates more pull and the tide is higher. The tidal bulge moves from east to west with the rotating earth and moon orbit. This usually leads to two high tides per day. Because it is 24 hours and 50 minutes from moonrise to moonrise, if it there is a high tide at 9:00 AM today, there will be another high tide at 9:50 AM tomorrow.

How does the tide affect the surf? It has a less to do with the movement of the water than with the slope of the bottom. Tide doesn't matter at beaches where the slope of the bottom changes little with depth. But that is rare. At some beaches, the bottom in deeper water is flat but steepens near shore. Low tides will cause spilling waves (good for learning) to break over the flat bottom. Intermediate tides will cause the waves to break over an intermediate slope, leading to plunging waves good for shortboarding. But high tides will cause the waves to break over a steep bottom, leading to surging waves that are suited only for bodyboarding or skimboarding. At other beaches, the bottom has the opposite change in slope with depth, again leading to the best surfing waves at intermediate tides. At reef breaks, the tide can be critical for submerging the reef to the ideal depth. If the reef is too submerged, waves won't break over it. Too exposed and the waves will break into the reef, instead of over it.

The right tide for surfing also depends on the size of the waves, because wave height will interact with the tide to determine what type of bottom the wave is breaking over. Usually, the ideal tide for big waves will be higher than for small waves.

Surfers commonly ask, "What's the tide doing?" Tides vary in amplitude from place to place and with the lunar and solar cycles, but at least you can look them up with a tide chart. Tide charts are available online, on your smart phone, or you can pick up an old-fashioned tide book for free at your local surf shop. If you'd rather spend money, there are several brands of waterproof watches that include programmable tide data. These can be a good investment if the tide has a big effect at your local break. But you don't need a chart, phone or watch to tell the tide. Low tide exposes marine animals and plants that live on rocky shores and pier pilings. If you can see mussels or algae, that's a sure sign that the tide is out.

Wind

Local winds can alter how good the waves are. The cleanest waves are on still, glassy days. If there is wind, the direction most favored by surfers is offshore (from land to sea). Offshore wind grooms the surf, holds up the wave face, and can make the waves hollow. However, strong offshore wind can make surfing difficult because spray gets in your eyes when taking off and the wind holds you up as you try to paddle down the face. Onshore winds (from sea to land) texture the surface of the water, making it difficult to ride on and paddle through. And if the onshore wind is strong enough, chop and small wind swells develop that disorganize the surf. Sideshore winds are less problematic than onshore winds. That said, surfing aerialists like onshore and side shore winds because it gives them lift and helps push them back into the face of the wave when they land. As a beginner, this is not something you need to worry about. The only air you will be getting is accidental.

Surfers time their sessions around the daily winds. Low-pressure troughs are created by hot rising air, and this sucks air from cold, high-pressure areas. This pressure differential leads to offshore winds in the morning and evening when the land is cooler than the ocean and onshore winds during midday when the land heats up. This is why experienced surfers try to get out early for dawn patrol, or come back late for an evening session.

Despite this general rule, the wind varies from beach to beach. A beach that faces one direction will have a different wind exposure than a nearby beach that faces another direction. For instance, on a stretch of beach with blown-out surf, the wind can be offshore just on the other side of a point. Or. if the point is formed by a tall headland, it will act as a windbreak. Even kelp beds can dampen the wind, leading to glassy waves despite whitecaps offshore. To score good conditions, you'll want to think about what the wind might be doing before you choose where to surf.

The surf's rhythms, melody, and cadence come from weather, the shape of the coastline, and the bottom topography. In our dance between human and water, the wave is the leader. Now that you know a little more about waves, you will be able to follow them better. In the beginning, it will be clumsy. You'll fall, step on some toes, and be cut in on. But, as you read further, you'll master the basic steps.

Wave Essentials

- *Wind creates swells.*
- *Swells have height and period.*
- *Swells break as waves in shallow water.*
- *Wave size increases with swell height and period.*
- *Wave faces can be measured in body-size units.*
- *Waves form at beaches, points, reefs, and reef passes.*
- *Human structures affect the way waves break.*
- *The tide and bottom slope change the shape of waves.*
- *Calm days or offshore winds are best for surfing.*

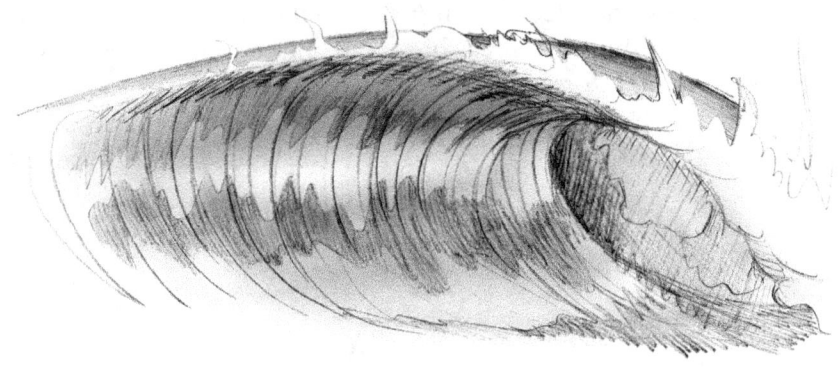

3. SURFBOARDS

Big Z: "Do you want to have your board with a lot of rocker or just a little?"
Cody: "I don't know."
Big Z: "What you want is something in-between. Trust me."
--*Surf's Up* (Columbia Pictures, 2007)

It's a cold but bright January morning, and I paddle out at a spot called Tarantulas on my 6'6. I've surfed this board for years in a wide range of waves, and this is the one I want under my feet when I take a steep drop. Large, lined up waves are breaking on a far reef. When I make it out, a couple other surfers are sitting at the reef, but they are riding boards a foot or two longer than mine. Then it dawns on me that the sets are even bigger than they looked from the sand. On my first take off, I realize that I don't have enough paddling speed to get into a wave before it pitches. I catch a few, but have a hard time setting my rail and carving turns. I remind myself to bring my gun next time a big, long-period swell hits this spot.

Later, as I'm resting on the beach, Tom Curren walks up. We chat about the waves and he asks how things went. I complain I was undergunned, and raise an eyebrow at the 5'10 he's holding. Then I watch, as the three-time world champion paddles out and tears the waves apart.

The right board for the job depends on the waves and the surfer's experience. At Tarantulas, I needed a bigger board, but Tom Curren, one of the most talented surfers ever, could have surfed it on a cafeteria tray. Although some shapes are better for learning than others, it is typical for a beginner to be more concerned about a board's color. Choose an appropriate board to learn on, add some wax to keep you from slipping off, and you are ready to hit the water.

Surfboard Anatomy

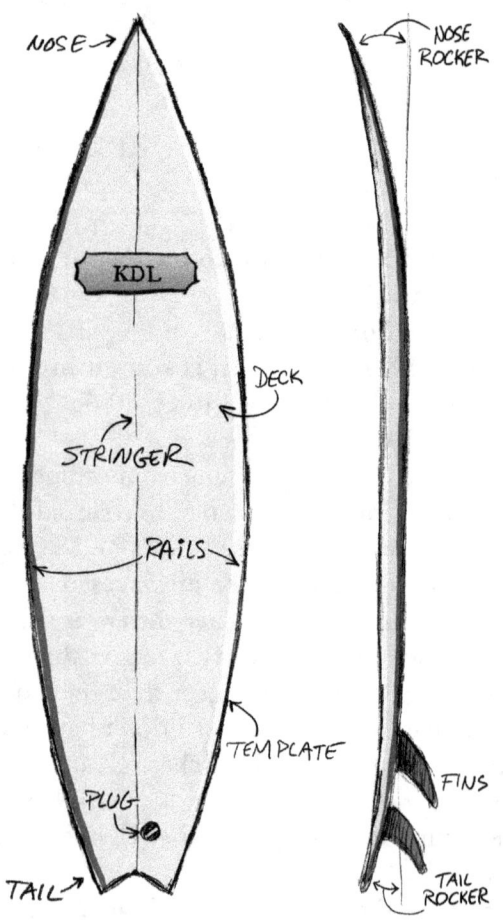

Imagine you are looking at a surfboard leaned up against a wall. Check out the board's length, width and outline. Around eye level, is a label that tells you who shaped the board. You'll also notice a wooden "stringer" for added strength, running down the centerline. At the upper tip of the centerline is the nose, and the tail is at your feet. Down near the tail, there is often a leash plug on the topside, or deck. More obvious, near the tail, but on the bottom of the board, are the fins or a skeg. Now grab the board's edges, otherwise known as rails. If you turn the board to look head on at a rail, you can see the curvature in the board's profile called the rocker. From the side, a board without much rocker looks like a piece of lumber. A board with a lot of rocker looks like a banana. Now, lift the board off the ground to see how little it weighs. Most surfboards have a thin fiberglass and resin coat that surrounds a core of light foam. The more foam in the board, the more water it displaces and the more it will float. Next time you walk into a surf shop, check out a bunch of boards this way. Be sure to read about their dimensions and caress their curves. But handle them carefully or you'll be shown the door.

Types of Surfboards

The Alaia

Early surfboards called alaias were planks of carved wood resembling an ironing board. The flat rocker of an alaia leads to a fast ride that, without fins, is difficult to control. Yet, the lack of fins allows for incredible freedom of sliding and spins. This makes riding prone on an alaia a great way to enjoy a small wave. Standing up an alaia, is far more difficult. The ancient Hawaiians who mastered surfing these boards must have been talented. Their chests were also probably full of splinters.

The Longboard

Longboards (or Mals/Malibus in Australia) dominated the golden era of surfing and have come in and out of vogue. Beginners surf them because their full nose, width (22-25"), and length (9-10') make for a stable platform. Their length also gives you room to touch your toes on the deck of the board as you lie down, giving you extra leverage when you pop to your feet. The best reason to learn on a longboard is they can catch small, mushy waves that are good for learning. Longboards carry a stigma of being old fashioned and for beginners. But they are also fun to surf in good waves, and make for a classic, stylish ride that can take years to perfect.

Shortboarders complain about longboarders being wave hogs. One reason longboarders get more waves is that a longboard is more efficient to paddle and can get a surfer to a peak faster than a shortboard can. And longboarders do not need to be in the steepest part of the wave to take off, enabling them to catch waves early. Also, because longboards paddle fast, longboarders are quick to get back to the lineup after riding a wave. These are all good reasons to learn on a longboard.

Longboards have some disadvantages. If you are small, you might find it difficult to get a longboard to the beach due both to its weight and it being too wide to carry under your arm. A longboard can also be difficult for kids and smaller adults to manage well in the water. Regardless of your size, a longboard can be difficult to paddle out through the surf (more on this topic soon). But, for most learners, these disadvantages are relatively minor, and longboards remain the board of choice for learning to surf.

The Big-Wave Gun
Guns (or big-wave boards) feature the pointy shape and narrow width of a shortboard but have the length of a longboard. Their length makes them easier to paddle into fast-moving big waves. Big-wave boards are more stable at fast speeds due to specialized rocker and rails that hold into the wave. But guns are not well suited for learning how to surf, and I won't go into more detail about them. Just be aware that if you see a big board for sale, don't buy it if it has two pointed ends unless you want a wall hanger. Otherwise, you will look like a fool flailing around in small surf with a big-wave board.

The Fish
A fish is a short, thick, and wide retro-shortboard, often with two fins (twin fins) and flat rocker. Flat rocker makes fish fast and ideal for small, mushy waves. Due to their width, fish are more stable and easier to paddle than modern shortboards, making them better to learn on. But twin fins give fish a loose and skatey feel. Modern fish, therefore, often have a small center fin for stability.

The Thruster
An Aussie named Simon Anderson shaped the first thruster in 1980. It was about his height, had a pointed nose, lots of rocker, and a squashed tail with three fins. The thruster allowed surfers incredible freedom on a wave, leading to the shortboard era. But these design features come at the cost of being harder to paddle and less stable than a fish, making them less suited for learning. Even though it is hard to learn how to surf on a shortboard, many young surfers with natural athleticism, balance, and perseverance, succeed in doing so. As long as you don't mind the struggle, learning on a shortboard is the most efficient way to get to the top of the sport.

The Funboard

A funboard (or mini-mal) is a hybrid between a longboard and shortboard. An appropriate size to learn on is about as long as you can reach over your head. For an average-sized adult, that's around an eight-foot board. The idea behind the intermediate length of a funboard is that it paddles like a longboard (sort of) and turns like a shortboard (sort of). As a result, funboards are good for beginners and can help intermediate surfers step from a longboard to a shortboard. However, because funboards have intermediate performance, advanced surfers shun them.

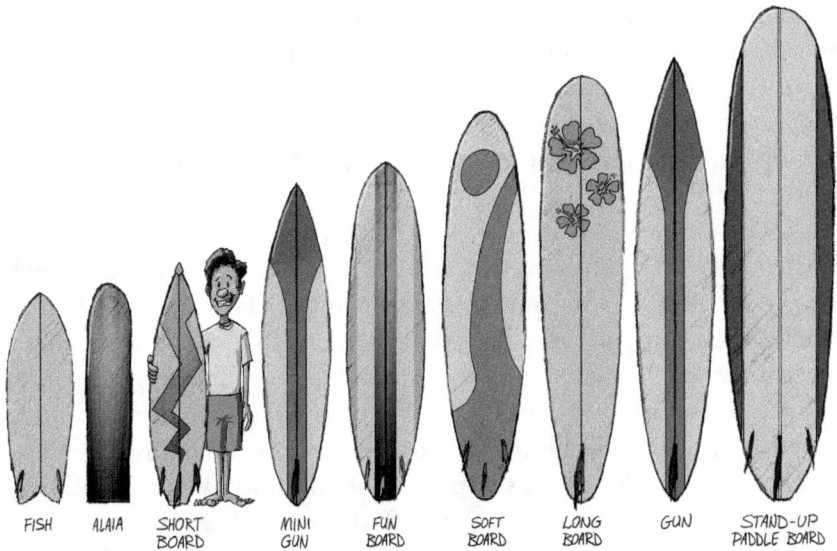

Types of Surfboards

The Softboard

The most popular choice for learners is an inexpensive softboard. Softboards (which are a funboard built out of bodyboard material) do not have an exterior shell of fiberglass and resin. Instead, they are made of waterproof foam. Soft foam increases safety and this gives parents confidence to buy their children softboards. Softboards also have the benefit of being more resilient to the abuse inflicted on them by a beginner. Safe and durable softboards are perfect for surf camps and beachside surfboard rentals. But there's a hitch. Softboards have the lowest performance of any type of surfboard. And, on a softboard, you are instantly identified as a beginner. After you've learned to surf, trade in your softboard for a surfboard built from foam, glass, and resin.

The Stand-up Paddleboard

The newest type of surfboard is the stand-up paddleboard (SUP). Stand-up paddleboards must be long, thick, and wide to allow a surfer to stand up on still water. When there are no waves, an SUP is a great way to enjoy the ocean. For instance, if the water is clear, you can view marine life while staying dry. Also, once you learn not to fall in, you won't need a wetsuit on an SUP.

And then, if you see a wave, you can try to catch it. Surfing even the tiniest waves with a stand-up paddleboard can be fun, and more and more stand-up paddlers are in the lineup. Partly, this is because an SUP can help extend the careers of surfers who, with age, find it hard to pop to their feet in time to catch a wave. I call my SUP my retirement plan.

Surfing an SUP is different from surfing a surfboard. Briefly, to catch a wave on an SUP, first practice until you can stay on your feet in a swell. When not paddling, try keeping the paddle in the water for a third point of balance. Your feet should be parallel with both toes pointed at the nose. Because you will be looking out to sea waiting for a wave, you need to learn how to turn the board rapidly when one comes. This is done by stepping back on the tail and paddling forward with short, wide strokes off the side of the board that is opposite to where you want to go. As the wave peaks, give a few hard strokes until the board begins to plane, and then switch into a surfing stance. This might sound easy, but it is harder than it looks (and it often looks ungraceful). To make things easier, SUPs shaped for surfing are shorter than those for cruising. Even so, SUPs have low performance on a wave. Therefore, unless you find the act of popping to your feet impossible, you are better off learning how to surf prone than with a stand-up paddleboard.

I should warn you, hopefully without prejudicing you, that all the reasons that shortboarders don't like longboarders apply twofold to stand-up paddleboarders in the surf zone. This means it is important for stand-up paddle boarders to take their turn and share waves with surfers. You will hear stand ups derisively called "sweepers", and other slurs. For instance, what do sharks call stand up paddlers? SUPper!

Buying a Surfboard

Do not buy a board before you try the sport a few times and decide you are ready to commit to it. In the mean time, you can try out a few different shapes suited for beginners at surf shops that rent boards. If you are unsure about what to choose, the shop employees can suggest a board that works for your size, abilities, and the local breaks.

Once you are ready to buy and know what board you want, shop for a used board. A good surf shop will carry used boards on consignment. You can sometimes find good deals at flea markets, garage sales, and local online For Sale ads. Plan on looking at several boards before you buy one. Keep in mind that if you don't make it clear you are a beginner, an over enthusiastic surf-shop employee can steer you to a high-performance shortboard. When I was learning, I overstated my abilities at the surf shop and walked out with a little thruster that barely floated me. I was stubborn and struggled through the next couple years catching few waves, and wishing I'd had less pride about buying a beginner's board.

Your first board should take you through the learning phase and into your first year of surfing, so it needs to be in decent shape. Start by evaluating the color for signs of weathering and damage. Then look for holes or cracks that show foam. These are most common on the nose, tail, and rails. Run your hands over the entire board to feel for uneven spots that betray dings that might not be obvious by eye. Then, check around the fin boxes for evidence of cracks or damage. Minor pressure dings on the deck or well-repaired dings can make a board ugly, but do not affect how the board will surf. If the board has a small ding, but the foam under the ding does not seem discolored, the board can still be a good buy if you fix the ding before paddling out. You might even get a discount if you point it out to the seller.

Beware of buying a used board with severe damage. Yellowing from sun exposure is a sign of neglect and weakened fiberglass (or glass for short). Weakened fiberglass can also appear as a bubble or soft spot where the glass separates from the foam due to compression from the feet. Such delamination spreads and is hard to repair. Don't buy a board with signs of it. Discolored foam near a ding means that water damage is deteriorating the board from within. This damage is also hard to fix. Avoid such boards, even if they seem cheap.

After a used board or two, you might want to buy a new surfboard. But like used boards, not all new surfboards are high quality. Surfboards used to be shaped by local surfers that would build custom boards for repeat buyers. Many shapers now generate a computer model of a surfboard, which is fed into a computer-controlled milling machine that cuts an almost finished blank out of foam. Often, unskilled workers, who have never seen a surfer, will sand and glass these machine-finished blanks in a distant factory. Such boards are often inexpensive because they are constructed with low-quality material. They might be in your budget, but they don't have much artistry and do not last long.

If you want a surfboard that merits the soul of the sport, look for a board hand-shaped by a professional you can meet in person. The shaper will ask about your weight and surfing skills before suggesting an appropriate length, thickness, rocker, and outline. In addition, the shaper will probably recommend a heavy glass job for a beginner. A total of ten-oz. of glass (the density/strength of fiberglass is measured in ounces), or at least a deck patch, will help prevent heel dings and delamination on the deck, and S glass and epoxy resin, though pricey, are more resilient to dings than standard fiberglass and polyurethane resin. This type of surfboard should get you through thousands of waves. But hurry, hand shaping is a dying art.

Waxing Your New Board
A wet surfboard deck is too slippery to stand up on. Before you can paddle out on a new board, you have to wax it. To wax a board, buy a couple bars of cold-water wax and a couple bars of warm-water or base-coat wax. First, clean and dry the deck of the board. The deck should be cool to the touch, so be sure the board is in the shade.

Protect the bottom by setting it on soft sand, carpet, or grass before applying the first coat. For the base coat, choose the warm-water wax. The high melting point keeps the base coat on your board, but the hardness makes it difficult to apply. To make things easier, warm up the wax first. You can put the wax in the microwave if you are in a rush, but the easiest way to warm wax is to carry a bar around in your pants pocket for half an hour. If you do it right, the bar is ready for waxing when you can barely squeeze it. Warm it even more and you can use it to prune your bikini line.

To apply wax for the first time, take the wrapper off the bar, hold it in your palm, and, starting at one end of the board, rub the wax on the deck (not the bottom!) in a 6"-8" diameter circle, slowly moving from one end of the board to the other. When you reach the end, reverse directions and reverse the circular motion. The wax should stick to the board in a pattern of dime-sized humps. Because longboarders often step up to the nose of the board, they wax their decks from tip to tip. However, you don't need to wax the nose of a shortboard, just the area from the tail to under the chest (about where the shaper usually places the deck label). Also, to reduce thigh rash (as discussed later), don't wax near the rails in the area you will sit. Furthermore, some surfboards have a foam traction pad over the tail that takes the place of wax (don't wax this). Once you have good coverage, and the wax humps are raised above the deck of the board, your base coat is ready. Don't forget to savor the tropical aroma of a freshly waxed board.

If the water is cold enough to wear a wetsuit, the base coat won't be sticky. You will need to apply a subsequent topcoat layer of cool or cold-water wax using the same technique. This wax will have a lower melting point than your basecoat, so it will be stickier, softer, and go on easier. Surfers often apply a new topcoat of wax before each session. But you don't need to wax every session when wearing booties, which have better traction than bare feet.

Now you can walk into a surf shop and buy or rent a board that is suitable for learning. As you improve, you can stick with your old board, or try something a little more advanced. Take care of a surfboard and you can ride it for years. After a while, you can accumulate a quiver of boards, each suited for a different wave type. How many is enough? Let's just say I'm not sure exactly how many I have.

Surfboard Essentials

- *A surfboard has a nose, tail, deck, bottom, and rails.*
- *Flat boards have little rocker and go faster but are hard to turn.*
- *Shapes include the longboard, shortboard, fish, funboard, and SUP.*
- *Funboards are the easiest shape to learn on.*
- *Start with a used board in good shape.*
- *Invest in a hand-shaped board after you learn.*
- *Wax your board to keep from slipping off.*

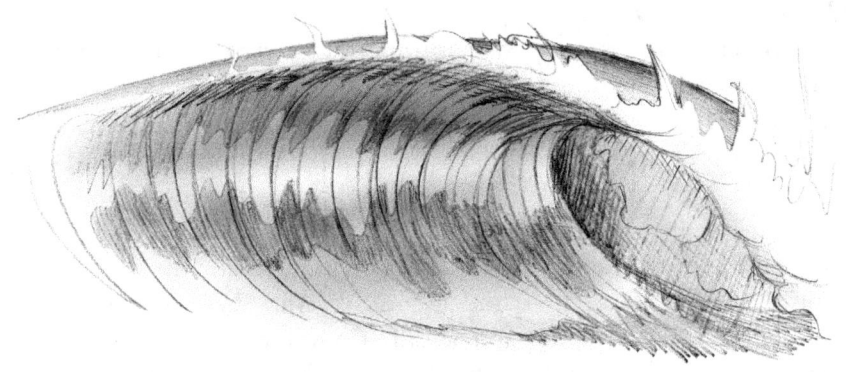

4. BOARD CARE

Jack: "Where's your surfboard?"
Matt: "In my car."
Jack: "Where's your car?"
Matt: "I don't know."
--*Big Wednesday* (Warner Bros., 1978)

When you look at a beater board, you can see the years of abuse: poorly repaired dings, yellowing from the sun, and delamination from the heat. Check out a rack of rental boards to get an idea of the punishment beginners inflict. But even a much-surfed board, if constructed well, can last decades if you follow a few important rules about surfboard care – the most important being, from personal experience, don't set it next to the bonfire.

There are many reasons to avoid dings. Dings take on water, which degrades the foam and adds weight. Damaged surfboards can be hard to repair yourself, and professional ding repair is expensive. Waiting on repairs might keep your board out of commission when a good swell is about to arrive. Eventually, you will want more than one surfboard, and the cost will add up if you cycle through boards too fast. Finally, because making a surfboard creates a lot of pollution, preventing dings will make your boards last as long as possible, reducing your environmental footprint.

Handle With Care

Most dings don't happen while surfing, they happen when handling. Carried boards get dropped and banged. This is especially true for beginners who might not be able to fit a board under their arms or find it heavy, dragging it along the sand, or dropping it on the pavement. Instead, carry your board by grabbing it in the middle, and keeping it tight to your body. Don't let the nose or tail dip down where it might scrape the ground. If it's windy, steady the board with your free hand to keep it under control. And when you set your board down, do it gently and avoid rocks and concrete. In other words, a surfboard is only a bit more durable than a chicken egg, so treat it as such, except for the scrambling part.

Do not expose your board to prolonged sunlight (or heat) as this can weaken the resin that holds your board together and take the flex out of the foam. Sunlight can also yellow a white board, which is a sure sign you either abused your board or picked it up cheap.

If you like your surfboard, invest in a bag. But don't just buy a cheap cloth board "sock". Socks only shield a board from the sun. To protect your board from both yellowing and dings, consider purchasing a padded travel bag. These bags are tough, but their weak spot is the zipper. Because zippers can corrode, you should rinse your board with freshwater before storing it in a bag. It's a drag when you pull out your board bag at the beach only to find you can't unzip it.

Transporting Your Board

Given that you will most likely be driving to the beach, you might want to know how to get your board into or onto a car. Don't start by leaning your board against the car. Invariably, the board will fall or blow over when you turn your back. Putting your board in the car will keep it out of the sun, safe from theft, and from sailing away at high speed. Most shortboards and funboards will fit into a passenger car if you follow these steps. First, be sure the board is dry. Then, lean the front passenger seat as far back as it will go (you might have to take the headrest off first). If your board is not in a bag, place a towel over the seat. This will help protect your car from melted wax. Now, from the hatchback or rear driver's side door, carefully slide the board, nose-first and deck up, to the floor of the passenger seat.

Place the board on the reclined seat so that it does not shift while driving (you can even secure it with a seatbelt). Your less important passengers can ride in back. Check to be sure that the board is not in contact with hard surfaces (if so, pad them with a folded towel). Finally, use a towel to cover parts of the board that will be exposed to sunlight for prolonged periods. Cars get hot in the summer sun. If you need to leave your board in the car, be sure to park in the shade and crack the windows open. Otherwise, the wax will melt on to your upholstery. Treat your board like you would your dog or sleeping grandmother, or better.

If you have a longboard, or don't want to take up space in your car, you will need to invest in roof racks designed for surfboards. You can buy hard racks that stay fixed to your roof, soft racks that you can remove after each surf trip, or pads and straps to convert a factory rack into a surf rack. Use straps that cinch down tight, not elastic straps or cords that will stretch with wind resistance. To reduce rusting your roof, rinse or dry the seawater off your board before racking it. Slide the board into its bag, then, place it deck down with the fins forward. If you stack boards on the rack and you don't have the boards in bags, place a folded towel between them to protect from dings and to keep the wax on the deck of one board from sticking to the bottom of another board. Cinch the straps tight and double check the ends to be sure they won't beat on your car roof as you drive. While driving, the taut straps can buzz and hum in the wind. Prevent this annoying sound by putting a single twist in each strap as you secure your board. Above all, double check that your boards are strapped in before you drive away. It doesn't take but a few seconds for unstrapped boards to fly off and hit the pavement.

You're fortunate if you can get to a surf break by bike. Unfortunately, cycling with a board under your arm and one hand on the handlebars is precarious. Even if you can master riding with your board, after a while, the arm holding the board will get tired. Resting your board on an unpadded handlebar is tempting, but will lead to a pressure ding on the rail when you hit a bump. To avoid this, you can pad your handlebars. Or, to make cycling with your board safer and easier, you can buy a specialized trailer for longboards or a bike rack for shortboards.

Water Hazards

The most common way to ding your board during surfing is to land on it with your knee or elbow. Get used to falling away from your board or landing with your palms out. That way, you will protect your board and spare yourself from bruises.

A collision with another surfer can easily ruin a board if a fin cuts into a rail, so stay away from crowded spots until you are confident that you know how to get out of the way in a hurry. I recall chatting with a friend in the lineup when I saw a set wave on the horizon. I sprinted to the peak, spun my board around and took off, only to run over him and his board. The six-inch gash in his board put him out of the water for a week. Come to think of it, I don't think we are friends now.

Dings can also stem from an improperly connected leash. Your leash connects to a leash plug with a thin cord tied in a loop. This thin cord, if it cinches around the rail during a wipeout, can cut through your board like a cheese slicer. To avoid this, make the leash loop as short as possible so it doesn't extend from the plug to the rail. Also, be sure you buy a leash that connects to the cord with a short piece of webbing (called a rail saver). This webbing expands the surface area of the leash at the rail, distributing the force when the leash wraps around your board during a wipeout. Surfing without a leash along a rocky coast is an even better way to get a ding. You will eventually lose hold of your board, and a board washed into shore always seems attracted to the sharpest rock on the beach.

A similar way to ding your board is by riding the whitewater to shore. This is where you are likely to hit a rock with your board or with your fin. If your fin hits a rock, it can sheer off, or, worse yet, transmit the force to the fin box or plug. This impact can crack your board and is difficult to repair.

So You Dinged Your Board

When, not if, you get a ding, leave the water as soon as possible and then fix it once the ding dries. But don't be tempted with a quick fix. Plugging the ding with wax just interferes with repairing the board later and, although duct tape can patch a ding for a session or two, if your board is dirty, wet, or salty, the tape will leak. You'll be better prepared for dings if you carry a tube of UV-activated resin with you. This allows you to patch up a small ding in the time it takes to make a cup of coffee.

Eventually, you will need to repair a major ding. With some guidance, you can learn to repair simple dings yourself. But you will need the service of a ding-repair specialist for large dings. Professional ding repair can be expensive but is usually worth the money. And once you fork out a nice dinner's worth of cash to repair a ding, you'll be a lot more careful with your board.

If you protect it, your board will maintain its flex, and light weight, perhaps gaining a few well-repaired battle scars. Then, when you grow out of your beginner surfboard, it will retain a bit of resale value, helping you to afford the next board of your surfing career.

Board-care Essentials
- *Surfboards are fragile.*
- *Take care when moving your board.*
- *Most dings occur on land, not in the water.*
- *Don't stand your board up.*
- *Keep your board out of the sun.*
- *Store your board in a padded bag.*
- *Transport with care.*
- *Fix dings sooner than later.*

5. WHAT TO WEAR

Penny: "You're going to surf in that?"
--Blue Crush (Universal, 2002)

The ancient Hawaiians surfed naked, but you will want to put something between your sensitive parts and the surfboard. Surfboards and wax create friction against your skin, sometimes the water is cold, and the sun will burn you. Fortunately, any decent surf shop sells surf trunks, bikinis, rashguards, and wetsuits to help you stay comfortable in the water, as well as leashes to keep you connected to your board after you wipe out. This is what makes surfing a $10,000,000,000 a year industry.

If the Water is Warm
If you are lucky enough to learn to surf in warm water, you don't need to wear much. Plenty of women surf in their bikinis. But a heavy wipe out can rip off a bikini, so choose one that fits well and snug, not one with flimsy ties, or decorations that will create drag. For guys, and many gals, the most basic surfwear is a pair of shorts. However, strong waves can rip off shorts with elastic waistbands. Even worse are walking shorts and cut offs that soak up water and become heavy. In contrast, modern surf trunks are designed for surfing. They are light, dry fast, and lack metal parts that corrode. Their pockets, if they have any, contain drains so they won't fill with sand or inflate with water.

Skin Care

There is a great feeling of freedom to "trunk it", but friction with the board can result in rashes and you'll be at risk to sunburn. A T-shirt is a good first step for added protection. Even better than a T-shirt is a thin rashguard designed for surfing. When buying a rashguard, look for a small loop sewn into the front of the hem. If you tie this loop into the drawstring of your surf trunks, the rashguard won't ride up above your waist when you wipe out.

Hats and sunglasses protect you from the sun on land, but they are impractical in the surf. Instead, invest in waterproof, greaseless (less slippery) sunscreen that won't sting your eyes. Dermatologists recommend sun protection factor 30 or higher with UVB and UVA blocking ingredients. Apply minutes before going into the sun, and reapply every few hours. Don't forget to add some extra sunscreen to the border areas of your swimsuit (e.g., above your butt crack) and the backs of your knees because these areas don't see a lot of sun, but get baked while you lie on your board.

Here's some rash advice. Surfers often get rashes under the armpits, around the neck, and on the chest and inner thighs. These rashes come from friction. To reduce friction, consider applying a skin lubricant (anti-chafe balm), like those made for triathletes. A cheaper, but messier, skin lubricant is petroleum jelly. Thigh and chest rashes develop because sitting and lying on a waxed surfboard rips your body hair out and forces the dirty wax into your hair follicles. Protect your hair follicles from getting waxed by wearing extra-long board shorts and a vest or rash guard. Also, don't wax the parts of your board that your bare thighs touch while sitting up. If you need additional thigh protection, wear a long pair of tight Lycra "jammers" under your board shorts. Should you get a rash, clean it with soap and water and then apply some diaper-rash cream so that it heals fast. Eventually, your rashes will fade and your skin will toughen up.

If the Water is Cold (Wetsuits)

Because water conducts heat better than air, if the water dips below 70° F (21° C), and you don't have much body fat, you are going to chill soon. When your core body temperature drops, it is harder to feel your fingers and toes, and your surfing deteriorates. This is why it is much more difficult to learn to surf in cold water. I once pulled into to a surf camp in Norway filled with ruddy-faced Swedes in thick wetsuits. Their secret was a wood-fired hot tub and a lack of any sensible beach for comparison. Kidding aside, wetsuit technology is opening a new frontier of surfing in high latitudes where there are still a lot more waves than surfers.

Even for warm water, you might invest in a one or two-mm neoprene vest. This will cut down on the wind chill and provide a little padding for your rib cage. But don't overdo it with the neoprene. Though thickness and coverage increase warmth, you're less agile when you wear a wetsuit because the added weight and tight fit make it harder to paddle and pop up. This means that you will need to reach a compromise between being warm or flexible – a tradeoff that depends on your cold tolerance.

How much wetsuit will you need? As the water cools below 70° F, you will see people wearing "shorties" or spring suits. These suits have two-mm thick neoprene and short arms and legs. They help keep your core warm without restricting you or adding much weight. Below 65°, many surfers opt for a three-two full-suit. This number means the suit is three-mm thick in the trunk and two-mm thick in the legs and arms. Below 60°, a four-three suit will help keep you warm, at least for a little while.

When the water temperature gets into the fifties, you will see surfers wearing booties to help keep their feet warm. In addition to insulating your feet, booties stick to the board better than bare feet (so you will need less wax), and they protect your feet when walking over rocks. Despite the advantages, a lot of surfers find booties clumsy. To stay agile, be sure to get the right type and size. The wrong types are dive booties, which are thick and clumsy, and reef walkers, which can slip off in the waves. In contrast, proper surf booties are thin, flexible, and have straps to keep them on your feet and minimize the influx of water. Surf booties often have a split between the big toe and the second toe that keeps your foot locked in place and adds a lot of dexterity. However, because this split can catch on your leash, look for surf booties that have a small bridge at the top of the split to block the leash. Once you've chosen the right type of bootie, pick a size that is a tight fit to keep your feet from sliding around inside. In surfing, small tight booties are better than big baggy booties. Also, be sure to tuck your booties under the leg cuffs of your wetsuit to prevent water from filling up the legs of your wetsuit. It's not easy to surf when each ankle is a giant water balloon.

85° - 70°   70° - 65°   65° - 60°   60° - 50°

Trunks and Wetsuits

If there is a chilling breeze, or if the air is cold enough that I can see my breath, I wear a neoprene hood made for surfing. You'll know you need a hood when you get caught inside on a big day and have to duck-dive waves until you get an "ice-cream headache" (or "brain-freeze") from the cold water. In addition to keeping you warm, a hood helps protect from surfer's ear (exostosis), a bony growth the body makes to keep the eardrum warm, but which can constrict the ear canal. Surfer's ear can be corrected with surgery, or turning up the volume on your stereo, but it is easier to wear a hood.

When it gets into the low 50s, surfers will switch to a five-four wetsuit and might put on neoprene gloves. Gloves interfere a little with paddling and popping up, but they help slow heat loss in cold water. As with other types of equipment, look for thin gloves designed for surfing, not SCUBA diving or dish washing.

Most surfers find a wetsuit more comfortable without a bathing suit on underneath. With a little practice, you will become adept at covering your nakedness with a towel while you change into and out of a wetsuit. When looking for a place to change, avoid dirt, or sand or oily parking lots. If you can't find a suitable spot, put down a towel or stand on your empty board bag. Some surfers bring a shallow plastic tub just for changing. A changing tub is also a good place to store a wet wetsuit after surfing.

Choose a wetsuit well. Most importantly, be sure it is a surfsuit. A thick dive wetsuit (these usually have a zipper in the front) will make it hard to paddle and pop up (and you'll look like a fool). To help you find your size, most wetsuit brands have a height/weight chart on the tag. Pick an appropriate suit and try it on. Because a wetsuit is only warm if it is tight, the material should hug all the contours of your body without any pockets or wrinkles. It should look like it was painted on but still allow you to breath and move normally. Modern surfsuits accomplish this by using elastic neoprene. The more expensive suits also have sophisticated ways to reduce water seepage, including zipperless entries that limit how much water can get in through your neck and back. Better suits also use blind stitching in the seams (so you can't see the stitches on the outside of the suit), as well as neoprene tape or glue covering the seams. All this technology adds up, and a good wetsuit can run almost as much as a new surfboard and not last as long.

Wetsuits are a big expense for a cold-water surfer. Unfortunately, time and use degrades the neoprene in wetsuits. You can extend a wetsuit's life by rinsing it in freshwater. After rinsing, a soaked wetsuit is heavy and drying it on a hanger or hanging it from the zipper cord will stretch it. To avoid stretching your suit, lay it on a deck, or drape it over a shower door till it dries. Once dry, store your wetsuit out of the sun so the materials don't degrade. As your wetsuit inevitably gets older and weaker, put it on and take it off carefully to keep from ripping it. With care, a wetsuit should last a couple winters, but once it has a few holes and rips, it's time to get another.
At some point (usually after a cup of coffee), you will need to pee while surfing. Because wetsuits don't come with a fly, if you don't want to interrupt your session, you are faced with a dilemma: stay or

go. Or is it go and stay? Hold it if you can, but if you own the wetsuit, don't stress over giving into nature's call. If you can't hold it, consider that urine is not that unsanitary and, as long as you rinse your suit well and take a shower, you won't stink up the place. The decision to pee while surfing is a matter of convenience balanced against your personal hygiene standards. My hygiene standards are pretty low; peeing in my suit has netted me hundreds of extra waves over the years.

Wear a Leash
Even though some old timers will scoff, beginners should wear a leash. A leash will spare you from swimming to the beach every time you fall off your board. You will fall a lot at first, and the leash will help you save energy for catching waves. More importantly, a leash also keeps the board from washing up on the rocks or hitting other surfers, especially scoffing old timers.

The leash connects from the tail of the board to a cuff that wraps around the surfer's back ankle (though some longboarders wrap the cuff under their knee). When attaching a leash to your ankle, be sure that the cord projects out from your body so that you don't trip on it while walking or surfing. And when you are carrying your board, hold your leash, or wrap it loosely around the tail, instead of dragging it behind you in the dirt. Leash dragging is classic beginner behavior.

Leashes come in different lengths and thicknesses. Shortboard leashes are around 5/16 inches (8 mm) thick and 6' (2 m) long. Longboard leashes are a few feet longer to let you walk the full length of the board and put more distance between you and the board when you wipe out. Eventually, you'll need a thicker leash for big waves.

Despite my suggestion that you wear a leash, don't rely on it. Your goal should be to stay connected with your board, not to ditch it at every convenience, and let the leash do the work for you. Think of your board like a well-heeled dog. Most of the time you won't need the leash; it's there for unforeseen situations only.

To conclude, surfing conditions change with the season and the weather. It will be harder to learn to surf if you are cold, rubbed raw, and sunburned. Know the water temperature before you paddle out or have a look at what the other surfers are wearing so you can copy them in the line up. Keeping warm, but not overly dressed, will help you learn faster and make your sessions more enjoyable.

Surfwear Essentials
- *Protect yourself from cold and friction.*
- *Use proper surf trunks.*
- *A rashguard will protect pale and sensitive skin.*
- *Choose the right wetsuit for the right temperature.*
- *Anticipate the need to pee.*
- *A leash will protect your board.*

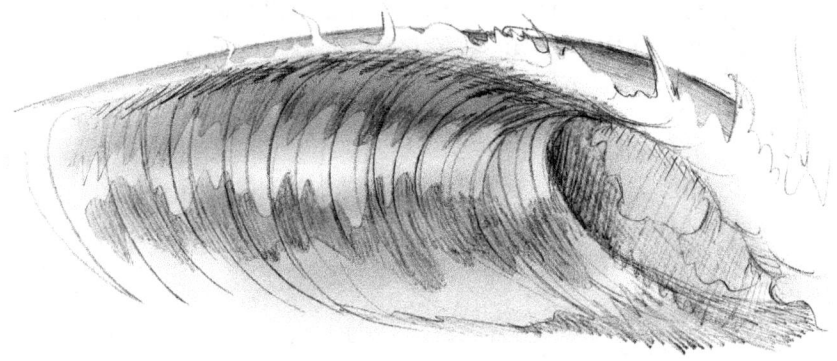

6. ETIQUETTE

Chino: "If you wanna surf the cove, you gotta earn it."
--*Lords of Dogtown* (Columbia TriStar, 2005)

Surfing has no official rules or referees, but it is far from anarchy in the line up. Before paddling out, you must know how we all get along. So here's a bit about surfing etiquette. Nothing that I talk about in this book is more important.

With the growth of surfing, beginners are outpacing retirees from the sport. There's already 20 million surfers, with more each year. This leads to crowds, and crowds can turn surf sessions into a frustrating hassle of jockeying for a few waves. Making the best out of crowds takes etiquette, respect, and generosity. Keep in mind that we are all in the water to have a good time and share some stoke.

Unfortunately, at a crowded break, you might see surfers taking off in front of other surfers that are already riding the wave. In the worst cases, one surfer drops in on another due to a false sense of entitlement stemming from localism, payback, or perceived superiority.

Right of Way
The golden rule of surfing is right of way. The right of way belongs to the surfer closest to the breaking section. Dropping in on another surfer with the right of way is the main source of scowls, cursing, and arguments in the water.

Sadly, dropping in on another surfer happens all the time. Sometimes it is a deliberate act of revenge, localism, or egotism. But more often, it is not. When two surfers are paddling for the same wave, it is not always possible to tell if the surfer with the right of way will make the wave. An experienced surfer who does not have the right of way, but has a good shot at the wave, will judge the difficulty of the wave and the priority surfer's ability and try to predict if the priority surfer will make the wave. If the priority surfer's chances look slim, the experienced surfer might paddle for the wave and drop in and then look back to see if the priority surfer is on the wave. When that happens, the surfer in front should then kick out of the wave to let the priority surfer finish the wave alone. On some waves, it is difficult to see if another surfer is coming down the line, and some surfers might drop in, mistakenly thinking the wave is free. If this happens to you, be sure to give a friendly shout to let the other surfer know that you are behind them. Or, if you hear someone yelling behind you on a wave, do your best to get off immediately. Then, be sure to apologize.

Dropping in on a Surfer that has Right of Way

A beginning surfer should always be conservative in crowded areas. Don't try to take off on waves that you don't think you will catch if there are other surfers that can. As Duke Kahanamoku said, "Just take your time - wave comes. Let the other guys go, catch another one."

There are cases where it's hard to tell who has the right of way. For instance, at some breaks, it is possible to go either right or left from the peak. If two surfers are going for the wave, they should split the peak. This requires calling out, for instance, "I'll go right, you go left." or "Let's split it." At other breaks, there can be two peaks with a single closeout section between them. This can put surfers on a collision course. In theory, the first surfer up has the right of way, but when in doubt, kick out.

When longboarders and shortboarders are surfing together, longboarders can paddle to a peak faster and get to their feet first. This means that shortboarders with the right of way can still be taking off after a longboarder with lower priority has already gotten to their feet and is surfing down the line in front of them. Here, the right of way is unclear and shortboarders and longboarders tend to differ in their views. Not surprisingly, many longboarders will say that the first surfer to their feet has the right of way. In my opinion, longboarders should pass on a wave if there is a shortboarder sitting inside that has right of way. On the other hand, shortboarders should avoid taking off on a wave a longboarder is already riding, and should definitely not paddle into the priority position while a longboarder is taking off.

Snaking

Right of way is easily abused. Some surfers will paddle around the surfer in priority position to get the right of way as a wave is forming. This is called snaking. Snaking can lead to more waves, and might seem like a good strategy, but it does not make friends in the line up. Here are a couple ways that snaking occurs. First, imagine two surfers waiting for a wave. A peak forms to the right of both. The surfer on the right has been sitting in priority position for this wave. But if the surfer on the left gets a head start and sprints to the right, this sprinting surfer might try to claim priority position as the wave begins to peak. As long as both surfers are able to take off on the wave, the sprinting surfer has snaked the surfer that originally had priority position. Even worse is when the snake paddles behind the back of the surfer sitting in priority position as a wave starts to form. The snake then takes the other surfer by surprise, sometimes leading to a collision. Not only is this unfair, it's dangerous.

Snaking is as annoying as cutting in line at the supermarket checkout. To avoid snaking, right of way should be established based on where surfers are sitting before the wave comes into view, not where they paddle once they see the wave. But even establishing right of way based on sitting can lead to conflicts where the takeoff spot is consistent from wave to wave. Here, any surfer can claim the right of way by moving a little closer to the peak than the rest of the pack. At such spots, surfers should take turns sitting in the priority position with those that have just paddled out heading to the back of the line. Unfortunately, most surfers can't count higher than about five, so taking turns falls apart when it gets crowded.

Don't be an Obstacle
Avoid paddling out where surfers are riding waves. Instead, start where it is uncrowded, and paddle until you pass through the surf zone before heading to the lineup. That way, surfers riding waves won't need to weave around you. However, when you wipeout or get caught inside, the wave often dumps you where other surfers are taking off. As the person inside, it is now your job to put distance between you and the face of the wave that is being surfed, even if it means getting pounded by the whitewater. Don't try to squeeze over a breaking wave by cutting in front of someone who is riding or taking off. Also, don't panic and ditch your board when a wave is bearing down on you. A leash is not an excuse to let go of your board. Loose boards are a hazard to others and all around bad form. If you are an obstacle, you might become a speed bump.

Keep a Low Profile
In practice, surfing etiquette applies differently to beginners. Experienced surfers will tolerate you as long as you keep a low profile and stay out of their way. If you are doing something annoying or dangerous, you can expect someone to give you a hard time. Do it twice and you might be asked to leave the water. This is not rude or unfriendly if the purpose is to avoid an injury.

There are social strata and pecking orders in surfing that you should be aware of. As a beginner, you are at the bottom of the totem pole. Good surfers, regulars, and locals are above you. Good surfers are admired for their talent and, as long as they are not snotty about it, tend to get cut slack about catching a lot of waves. If you do become a good surfer, try not to abuse that privilege. The most hated person in the water is a good surfer who is a jerk about it. If you go to a beach a few times, you will begin to notice some familiar faces. These are the regulars that surf the spot a lot. They are dedicated surfers and will chat about last week's swell or the dip in water temperature, or the wind forecast for the afternoon. They are a good source of facts about where and when to surf. Regulars are often locals, but not necessarily. Locals are the folks who live near the surf spot (i.e., don't need to drive there). Locals might not be regulars. They might have busy work schedules or family lives and not get to surf as much as they would like. Nonetheless, locals can tell you about the history of the area, its geography, and local color. This knowledge can help you learn faster and gain confidence with the crowd.

Because waves are a limited resource, visiting surfers, experienced and beginner alike, compete with the locals. In particular, locals look down on anyone else that acts like they own the place. Captain Cook (or Captain Kook as they probably referred to him), got chopped into small pieces for being a jerk. Had Cook shared with the locals instead of shooting at them, things probably would have worked out better for him. Although nobody has a right to keep you from surfing, beginners should avoid localized spots. It's hard to learn if you are worrying about the neighborhood delinquents slashing your tires.

It takes time to earn respect in the water. You might be in the right spot for a wave, only to have a more experienced surfer snake you, or drop in on you. It's a drag to get burned like this, but expect it to happen if you are not surfing well. You were probably disrespected because an experienced surfer watched you blow your last three takeoffs, and grew tired of having you take the priority position, only to let a wave go unridden. This is yet another reason to avoid crowded areas when you are learning.

How do you know if the crowd will be a factor? You can't always tell by the number of people in the water. Signs that a break is too crowded for learning to surf include multiple surfers paddling for the same wave or people yelling at each other in the water. But don't be dissuaded by a crowd if most are beginners or if the atmosphere seems lighthearted. Instead, paddle out and add to the positive vibe.

Keep the Beach Clean
Surfers have little patience for those that damage the beach. The beach, including the local wildlife, like shorebirds and marine mammals, deserve your respect. This means knowing the rules about driving on the beach or having pets. Most of all, don't litter. Anyone that leaves broken glass, cigarette butts, or lets their dog crap on the beach deserves to be asked to leave. Instead of causing problems, pick up some trash and leave the beach cleaner than when you arrived. To make a difference at your beach, get involved with your local chapter of the *Surfrider Foundation*.

There are unstated rules in surfing, like there are stated rules in a library, bowling alley, or cockfight. We expect you to know the rules and follow them. Don't litter, don't ditch your board, and keep out of our way. Most importantly, the surfer sitting closest to the curl has the right of way. Does this rule get broken? All the time. Should you break it? Never.

Etiquette Essentials
- *Yield to surfers with right of way.*
- *Don't snake to get priority position.*
- *Don't obstruct another surfer's ride when paddling.*
- *Don't ditch your board.*
- *Apologize when needed.*
- *Know your place.*
- *Respect the beach.*

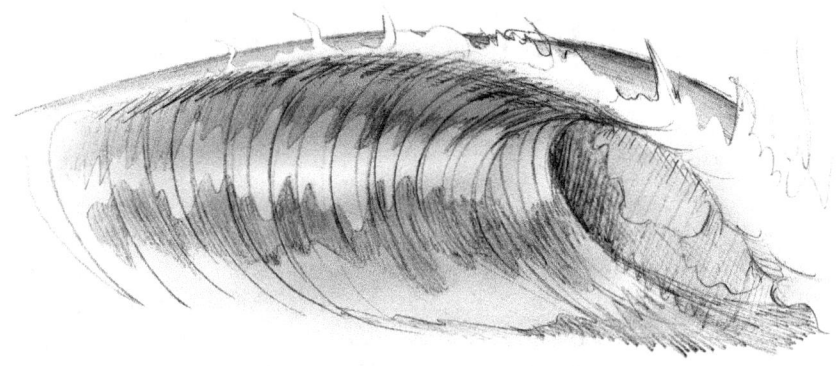

7. SAFETY

Kilgore (explosions in the distance): "If I say it's safe to surf this beach, captain - it's safe to surf this beach."
--Apocalypse Now **(American Zoetrope, 1979)**

We are land creatures and the ocean can be an unforgiving place to visit. Big waves and strong currents can hold you under, take you out to sea, or drive you into the bottom. Some marine animals can hurt you and some places have water-borne diseases. More commonly, you can collide with your own board or with other surfers. The list of hazards is long, but you can surf safer if you are aware of the risks.

The most common surf-related injuries are cuts to the head, lower leg, and foot due to hitting boards or the bottom. Bad wipeouts can also lead to sprains to the back, knee, and ankle, or broken legs, ribs, and noses. Slapping your head against the water as you go over the falls can perforate an eardrum. But you don't have to wipeout to hurt yourself. Paddling a lot can strain the shoulders, back, neck, and elbows, and chronic rashes can develop on the armpits, knees, and torso. My most frequent injuries over the years have been rotator cuff damage, a broken nose from smashing my face into my board, and cuts from fins. But this is minor compared to my friends that have been dragged over coral reefs, broken legs, or severed blood vessels to the point of near death. Although surfing injuries are rarely fatal, a surfer dies at my local breaks about once a decade.

Fitness

Above all, surfing requires stamina and water skills. You should be athletic and a confident swimmer. If you are out of shape, you'll soon become exhausted in the water, and this can create a safety hazard for yourself and others. Please stay on the beach instead.

Being in good shape isn't enough to start surfing. You also need to have some experience with waves. Please don't try to surf on your first-ever trip to the beach. The ocean is a formidable environment and you will need to be at ease in it to focus on learning to surf. If you are new to the ocean, spend some time playing in the waves, body surfing, or riding a bodyboard before attempting to ride a surfboard. As a rule, avoid situations that are outside your psychological or physical comfort zone.

Hitting the Bottom

Although some waves break over hard rock and coral reefs, it is rare for experienced surfers to be injured by hitting the reef. My home break is rocky and I've had thousands of wipeouts, but never more than a bruise from hitting the rocks. This is because the rocks are smooth and have soft algae growing on them. Other reefs are less forgiving, especially those with barnacles, rock oysters, or coral.

Some of the best waves in the world break over shallow coral reefs. When I surf these spots, I always wear my reef booties to protect my feet. Just one poorly timed wipeout on a heavy wave can leave you standing on a reef of live coral that can slice you to ribbons. If you get more than a shallow coral cut, seek medical attention. Even if it is just a scrape, be sure to wash it well to get rid of debris and then apply antibiotics. Reef cuts easily become infected, especially in wet and humid weather, and, in rare cases, this can be life threatening. I was on a return flight from a surf trip to Indonesia and one of the surfers on my plane had a week-old reef cut on his arm that had started to fester. By the time we'd reached our layover stop in Japan, he went into septic shock and was rushed to a hospital.

To avoid hitting the bottom, note the depth. A few inches of water is enough for surfing, but you need more than a couple feet of water to fall safely, and several more feet if you are tumbled by a good wave.

Even if the water seems deep, don't dive head first as you fall from your surfboard. Instead, fall horizontally back into the white water. Then try to sink with your feet or butt first. If you do find yourself falling head first toward the bottom, extend your hands to cushion the blow.

You'd use a helmet snowboarding or mountain biking to protect your head from a fall. Hitting your head is even more dangerous in the water than it is on land. A couple years ago, at the beach where I live, a teenage girl hit her head surfing, went unconscious and drowned before she could be pulled from the water. Surf helmets might seem over the top, but they are a smart investment. Investors in my friend's company worried about losing him in a surfing accident and had him sign a contract stating he would always wear a surf helmet. It took him a while to get used to it, but now it is second nature and he wouldn't surf without it, contract or no contract.

Watch out for shallow, rocky areas inside the breaking waves. Getting caught inside during a big set on a shallow reef can leave you banged up and stressed out. I once was caught inside at a Mexican break called Todos Santos. Two set waves pushed me, exhausted, up to an urchin-studded cliff. One more wave would have beached me on the rocks with no exit. But I caught a break in the set, paddled through the boils and whitewater back into the lineup, and chose my waves more carefully thereafter.

The most common way to get hurt on a reef is walking in shallow water. Here, a misstep can cause you to slip and fall, cut your foot, or twist your ankle in a crevice. It's a good idea to plan your entry and exit, move slowly, and wear booties. Sometimes you will see surfers wading gingerly over a rocky reef while pushing down on their floating surfboard. Pushing down distributes the surfer's weight to the board, reducing the force of contact between the feet and the reef. This trick lowers the chance of being cut by a rock or impaled by a sea urchin. Better yet, look for a sandy patch in the beach to walk over. I eventually tired of walking the reef at my home break, so I scouted the beach at low tide and memorized the channels and sandy spots. Those easy entry and exit points have saved my feet and boards over the years.

Hazardous Marine Life

Beneath the waves is a merciless food web. Animals are busy eating and trying not to be eaten. Stick one toe in the water and you can get caught in the crossfire. It's a battle zone out there and you'll want to know who the combatants are and how to protect yourself from them.

Sharks

In the fifties, my friend was surfing at his home break on Oahu. He caught a wave, and paddled back, only to find half a board and a slick of blood where his friend had been sitting. Even after describing to everyone what had happened, the death was reported as a drowning by the press. The newspapers back then were busy protecting Hawaii's image as a safe place for tourists to come to play in the ocean. But tiger sharks can be common near coral reefs, and they hunt people as well as sea turtles, sharks and manta rays. Given that menu, you can see how surfers might seem like an easy snack to a tiger shark. In contrast, and despite what Peter Benchley wrote in the novel *Jaws*, great white sharks don't seem to hunt humans specifically, they sometimes mistake us for the seals and sea lions that are their normal prey. It's easy to imagine how, from below, a paddling surfer looks like a fat, spastic seal to a great white shark. Other shark species attack people. Most notably, bull sharks and sand sharks bite surfers in warmer water over sandy bottoms and near rivers. But your odds of seeing a shark, let alone being bitten by one, are slim and not worth obsessing about. Some estimate the odds of being attacked by a shark at one in twelve million. And most of those attacks are not fatal.

There are a few things you can do to reduce your odds of a shark attack. Sharks are attracted to blood, so get out of the water if you are bleeding. And stay away from fishing piers where people are cleaning their catch. Furthermore, if there are many seals and sea lions in the water where you surf, listen for stories of shark sightings. At sharky spots, avoid surfing alone (because you will need assistance if you are bitten), and also be more cautious at sunrise or sunset when sharks are more likely to be foraging and mistake a surfer for a proper meal.

When a fatal shark bite happened recently near one of my favorite surf spots, the local surfers were understandably on edge. The next week, I paddled out and saw half a bloody seal floating in the surf zone, a sure sign that a great white had been foraging. But such obvious signs of sharks are rare. When in doubt, don't go out. For instance, during a contest heat in the sharky waters of Ocean Beach in San Francisco, pro surfer Dusty Payne saw a big fin coming straight at him. It scared him enough that he paddled in. Although he forfeited his round, he lived to compete another day.

Please don't hate sharks because you fear them. Humans have less to fear from sharks than sharks have to fear from humans. For every shark that kills a human, humans kill ten million sharks. In particular, a growing appetite for shark-fin soup has led to overfishing. When diving on fished reefs, I'm lucky if I see a shark a week, but on similar unfished reefs, I've counted a hundred sharks in an hour. I've had sharks approach me out of curiosity, and a little one bit my ankle once, but they've never hurt me. In person, these sharks are magnificent animals that show no malice. And, like lions or grizzly bears on land, sharks play key roles in the ecosystem, such as weeding out sick prey. Sadly, the global massacre of sharks is unraveling the marine food web, turning a once wild ocean to a simpler and less exciting one. But that's a sad end; how about a joke? What do sharks call human children? Appetizers!

Stingrays
Sharks might be intimidating, but injuries from stingrays are much more common. Lifeguards report that stingrays injure about 500 people at southern California beaches each summer, especially in warm water near harbors and estuaries. In such habitats, stingrays bury in the sand out of sight. Unaware waders can accidentally step on a stingray, which then gets upset and lashes out in defense with its tail, striking the surprised swimmer's foot or lower leg with a venomous barb. Being stuck by a stingray is unlikely to kill you, but the wound and the injected venom hurts like a hundred bee stings. To keep your sessions stingray free, stay on your board. When wading, shuffle toe-first across the sand to frighten off stingrays before you step on them.

In the case of a stingray puncture, get the victim to land and apply pressure to reduce bleeding. To manage the pain, soak the wound in hot water for a couple hours to help neutralize the venom (peeing on it won't help). Then, clean the wound with soap and water. Meanwhile, if the injured person is dizzy or has difficulty breathing, call for medical assistance. While waiting for help, try to determine if part of the barb is still in the wound and wash it out if possible. If there is any chance that part of the barb is still in the wound, go to a hospital to have it removed. Otherwise, there is a high risk of infection that can be worse than the sting.

Marine Mammals
Nothing says beginner like a surfer screaming, "Shark!" and paddling in as a dolphin passes. The most distinguishing feature of a shark is that both the dorsal and tailfin are vertical. You will often see two fin tips breaking the water as the shark glides by. Dolphins, however, have horizontal tails (flukes) and break the surface in an arc when they come up for a breath. Get these signs straight, and you won't make a fool of yourself. Or, do it intentionally and clear the water of beginners.

That's not to imply that dolphins want to be your friend. Some dolphins play and ride waves in the lineup and have hurt curious surfers and swimmers by accidentally (so we assume) landing on them. If you see a bunch of dolphins jumping in the surf, enjoy the view, but don't risk paddling over to get a better look.

In colder water, it is common to see seals and sea lions (pinnipeds). Harbor seals are nosey, and can scare you half to death by popping up suddenly, or nuzzling your feet. Otherwise, harbor seals are not a threat. In contrast, during breeding season, large male sea lions and elephant seals become territorial. Their bite is worse than their bark, so take the hint if they seem annoyed with you. This is your cue to back off. A kneeboarder I know from Oregon suffered the interest of a hormonal seal when it attempted to mate with him (sending my friend to the hospital with a lot of explaining to do). And definitely don't approach marine mammals on the beach. On land, pinnipeds feel vulnerable and will defend themselves by biting.

Urchins

Sea urchins are rock-dwelling invertebrates with sharp spines. The spines of most sea urchin species can penetrate human skin and the resulting wounds can become infected. Obviously, avoid walking barefoot on reefs covered with urchins. If sea urchins are common on a reef, the local surfers will know and, if asked, can point out areas to avoid.

If you do get stuck by sea urchin spines, soak the area in hot water and try to remove the spines with tweezers. Then clean the wound with soap and water and apply an antibiotic cream. However, it's not always easy to get the spines out. I have several purple spots in my palms and feet where sea urchin spines have broken off and left tattooed reminders of being impaled.

Jellyfish

Many jellyfish species are not a bother, at most causing a brief sting and rash. But some, like the box jellyfish in northern Australia, can be deadly and hard to see. And others, like the fist-sized Portuguese man o' war, are simply painful. When I first surfed amongst man o' war in Senegal, I was nervous about getting stung. But a local surfer showed me that the floating jellies were easy to avoid and that my wetsuit protected me from the tentacles.

If you do get stung, don't rinse off the tentacles with freshwater as this causes the stinging cells to release. Again, don't pee on the sting. Instead, remove jellyfish tentacles with tweezers or tape. You can also use vinegar to neutralize the sting and then soak the injured area in hot water for 30-90 minutes to reduce the effect of the toxin.

Seaweed

Some people have an irrational fear of touching seaweed. Seaweed is not dangerous, but large floating "kelps" can be annoying if they interfere with riding or paddling or by wrapping around the surfer's leash. When surfing in kelp, try to tuck your leash between your board and body to keep it from dragging and being snagged when you paddle or are waiting for waves. Entanglement in kelp can be frustrating, but be patient and you'll pull free.

Surf Hazards

Water Quality

Bacteria and viruses wash into surf breaks via rivers, sewage outflows, and storm drains. Studies show that exposure to water near storm drains carries a higher risk of getting an upper respiratory or gastrointestinal infection. More serious health concerns, like Hepatitis A virus, can be common in some developing countries that don't have the wealth or infrastructure to treat their sewage. Even in wealthy countries, a strong rain can flood the sewer system, spilling the overflow into the ocean. From there, human viruses can travel miles with the currents. Surfers have a selfish interest in clean water, and groups like *Surfers Against Sewage* and the *Surfrider Foundation* have been instrumental in passing and enforcing clean-water laws. Please don't tell them I said you could pee in your suit.

Some places will post warning signs if water testing indicates high levels of indicator bacteria (e.g., fecal coliforms). But because water-testing programs often lack funding, and testing can lag behind contamination events, it's best to follow some common-sense rules to stay healthy. Avoid surfing at river mouths and near sewage outfalls. And health officials suggest that surfers stay out of the water for a couple days after a heavy rain. But don't assume that the water is clean because there are surfers in the lineup. If the waves are good, many surfers will get wet even if there are health risks. There is no IQ test for surfing.

Surfboard Dangers

The most dangerous animal you will surf with is yourself. This is because surfboards, though fragile, have hard, pointed ends. In particular, the back edge of a surfboard fin is sharp as an axe, and it can cut through a wetsuit and, sometimes, into skin. A friend of mine almost died of blood loss on the North Shore of Oahu after her fin sliced deep into her leg during a wipeout. Another barely survived a similar accident at a remote Mexican beach. I once gashed open the back of my ankle while duck diving. I was still bleeding when I got back to the beach an hour later and, when I bent over to take off my leash, almost passed out from blood loss. If you do cut yourself, get to shore, apply pressure, and elevate the wound to help stop the bleeding.

Fortunately, many beginner's boards have fins of flexible plastic that can't cut your skin. Some fin manufacturers make fins for regular boards with softer edges that are much safer to surf with yet don't cut down on performance. Look into these fins whether you are a beginner or expert. If you already have a set of fins, or your fins are glassed on, chances are they are unnecessarily sharp. Use sand paper to dull the edges and points until you don't think you'd mind the fin slashing into your face or leg.

The next most dangerous part of your surfboard is a pointy nose. Fortunately, you can buy a flexible nose guard that will bend instead of impaling you. In addition to increasing safety, a nose guard protects your board from getting dinged up during transport and storage. A nose guard won't reduce the performance of your board and should be standard on any sharp-nosed shortboard.

Beware of Your Leash

Leashes can snag on rocks and algae, and this can trap a surfer under water. This is rare, but at one of my regular breaks, there is a memorial to a young mother who got her leash wrapped around a rock during a big swell. The long-shore current was so strong that it pulled her under and, unable to free herself, she drowned.

Fortunately, leashes connect to your ankle with a Velcro wrap that is easy to rip off. But you're probably not going to be able to see your leash cuff in an emergency, and you won't have much time to grope around for it. You can make this easier if you memorize how you wrapped the leash cuff around your ankle so that you can rip if off without looking. That's why I always wrap my leash cuff clockwise. Because my right foot is my rear foot, if I find the grab-tab at the end of the cuff with my left hand, I just pull it toward my body. If you are goofy-footed, the opposite wrap will work for you. Also, as a habit, when I come back to shore, I practice taking my leash off without looking.

Another danger is that a leash can loop around a body part during a wipe out. Waves can pull a board underwater with force enough to severe a finger or toe. And you certainly don't want that force to close around your neck. Perhaps I'm paranoid, but if I feel my leash up around my head during a wipeout, I put my arms up against my face to provide a barrier to a potential noose. If I'm going to hang, it better be for a good reason.

A third danger of a leash is that it acts like the string on a yo-yo, pulling your board back to you. If the leash stretches and contracts, the board can snap back and hit you. So test a new leash to be sure that it is not elastic. Jack O'Neil, inventor of the surf leash, learned about elastic leashes the hard way when his surgical-tubing leash snapped back and rocketed his board into his face. As a result, Jack now sports an eye patch. Modern leashes are safer, but boards still come flying back. Unless you've yearned for the pirate look, anytime you surface, be sure to put a hand in front of your face. This way, your board will hit your hand instead of your head, and you can save your eye patch for Halloween.

Collisions

Other surfers can run into you or get in your way while you are surfing, and collisions are the next most likely source of injury for surfers. Getting hit by the nose of another surfer's board or run over by their fins can be even more dangerous than colliding with your own board. In particular, longboards, stand-up paddleboards, and surf kayaks have a lot of momentum on a wave and can be difficult for a rider to steer. When one of these is headed toward you, try your best to get out of the way, either by moving to the side or diving deep.

A common place for a collision is when one surfer is paddling out through a breaking wave at the same time another surfer is coming down the face. The next most typical place for a collision is when two surfers try to take the same wave. Surfers minimize collisions with knowledge of and respect for surfing etiquette. Irrespective of etiquette, it is a good idea for beginners to avoid crowded areas so that they don't cause collisions either through ignorance or from being out of control. Nothing will get you yelled at quicker than causing a collision that injures a person or dings a board.

Myelopathy

There is a rare, but serious, medical disorder that can strike beginning surfers called Surfer's Myelopathy. When the surfer lays prone with the head up and then moves to pop up to their feet, hyperextension of the back can kink a blood vessel and this can cut off oxygen flow to the spine. The resulting damage varies, from temporary loss of feeling in the legs to permanent paralysis. Fortunately, this has only been documented a few dozen times. Even though Surfer's Myelopathy is rare, beginners need to be aware of the signs so that they will know to stop surfing if their legs feel numb. I learned about Surfer's Myelopathy first hand because one of my daughters showed symptoms while learning to surf. In her case, the risk of paralysis has kept her from surfing.

Hold Downs

If you surf long enough, you will eventually get pounded by a big wave, such as when an outside set catches you by surprise and breaks on you. You can minimize getting caught inside by watching the waves before you paddle out and getting an idea for where the larger sets are breaking. But when you do get caught inside, you can lessen the punishment by getting under broken waves. The deeper you duck dive or turn turtle (or Eskimo roll, see below), the more you will avoid the turbulence of the breaking wave and the easier it will be to return to the surface. Holding on to your board will also give you buoyancy that helps you float back to the surface. It's your parachute in reverse.

If you get caught up in the turbulence, don't panic. A big wave can keep you underwater for a few seconds, but most surfers are able to hold their breath for at least a minute. Still, more than ten seconds without a breath can seem unbearable, especially if the wave is spinning you around. When spinning, try to shield your head with your arms. You won't be able to see the bottom and might not even have a clue where the bottom is. Relax your body, protect your head, and remember that you can hold your breath for a long time. Once you stop spinning, get a bearing on where the surface is and head up to it. If you are near the bottom, pushing off with your feet will propel you faster to the surface. Your board will be headed to the surface too, and you can sometimes use your leash as a guide. If you can't find the bottom, stepping on your taut leash gives you something to push against on your way to the surface. The instant your head breaks the surface you will want to breathe, but be aware that waves and chop on the surface can sometimes trick you into sucking in water or foam. It's better to wait to breath until your head is well above water and your eyes are open.

The moment you get that breath, look out for the next wave. Hopefully, you will get a second or third deep breath before having to dive again. Doing this for five or six waves in a row is exhausting. If you are not in excellent shape, avoid days with consistently large waves.

Currents

High surf, tides coming in or out of bays or estuaries, and the flow of rivers into the ocean can set up strong currents. A current makes it difficult to wait for waves and can require constant paddling just to stay in one place, like walking the wrong way up an escalator. This is fatiguing, which can be dangerous in large surf where you might need to hold your breath over and over.

In the shallow water inside of the breaking waves, a long-shore current can form. This current sweeps in the same direction that the waves approach the beach. The higher the surf, and the more the waves hit the beach at an angle, the stronger the long-shore current can be. Although, this current fades outside of the surf zone, it can mess with you as you start to paddle out. Paddling out on a big day at Bells Beach in Australia, a raging long-shore current pulled me a kilometer, nearly to Winkipop Point, before I could get through the surf zone. When the long-shore current is strong, entering and exiting the water up current of the lineup is a good strategy. Also, note where on the beach you paddled in from so that you know how far you might have drifted. And be careful about currents that will pull you into hazardous rocks, piers, or other structures.

A temporary current flowing from the beach out through the waves is called a rip tide (they have nothing to do with the tide). Rip tides occur after a set of large waves scours a hole in the sandy bottom, causing the water retreating off the beach to funnel into a channel through which more and more water flows. Fortunately, rips are easy to see because they are choppy and carry a lot of sand and foam with them. To get out of a rip, don't bother paddling against it. Paddle up or down the coast until you reach calm water. Because waves do not break well against a rip tide, experienced surfers will use rips as an easy way to paddle from the beach through the surf zone.

Rescues

At most surf breaks, professional help is far away. Other surfers will be your best source of assistance, paddling you to shore and administering CPR if needed. You can prepare yourself to help other surfers by knowing basic life saving, watching for surfers in trouble, and learning CPR. Once, while surfing at Morro Rock in central California, I watched five guys dare each other to jump into the cold water. Three swam to shore, but two were weak swimmers and got caught in a rip current. When it became clear that they were headed out to sea, a friend and I were able to paddle over to them and use our surfboards to get them back to shore. It turned out those fools were friends of ours.

But be cautious about rescuing people. Struggling swimmers can panic and push you under in their desperate attempts to get a breath, and untrained rescuers can end up as victims. If you find someone panicking in the water, don't risk your own life trying to rescue him or her. Instead, alert a trained lifeguard. A lifeguard will keep their eyes on a victim as they paddle or swim to them, while simultaneously being aware of hazards, like rocks, currents and breaking waves. The victim can then be given a float so that they don't cling to the lifeguard. If the victim is unconscious and not breathing, the lifeguard can give rescue breaths in the water until they reach the beach where the guard can administer CPR.

If you find someone unconscious, get him or her to shore or on a surfboard and assume they are drowning. All drowning victims require emergency assistance from medical professionals. Assign someone to call for medical help while you stay with the victim. If the victim is breathing, place them in recovery position (on their side) to keep their airway clear and free from vomit. If they are not breathing, time is of the essence to save their life. Immediately seek someone trained in CPR to begin rescue breaths and chest compressions. This will help circulate blood and expel water from the lungs. If the victim breathes again, keep them warm until help arrives. As a beginner, you are less likely to make a rescue than to need rescuing. Don't surf alone and preferably surf in view of a lifeguard. But a lifeguard is not a substitute for good judgment. Never paddle out if you feel insecure. Surf with a friend or two, and watch each other.

You can surf safe. Although many novice surfers focus on rare threats like sharks, most injuries occur when surfers collide with their own board or run into other surfers. Fortunately, there are lots of things you can do to minimize your risk of injury. When beginning, choose equipment that has fewer sharp edges, like a softboard. And use a leash, but know how to remove it. If you fall or get caught inside by a set, don't panic. Instead, protect your head and let the spin cycle play out until you can float back to the surface for a breath. Most importantly, carefully assess the conditions. Don't paddle out into strong currents, large surf, or rocky reefs before you are ready.

Safety Essentials
- *Be in shape.*
- *Be comfortable in waves.*
- *Know the bottom type.*
- *Avoid urchins and rays.*
- *Stay out of polluted waters.*
- *Use a nose guard and soft-edge fins (or sand your fin edges).*
- *Know how to take off your leash.*
- *Avoid strong currents.*
- *Relax during hold downs.*
- *Protect your head.*
- *Avoid collisions.*
- *Learn first aid and CPR.*

8. GETTING READY

"..And when the DJ tells me that the surfin' is fine, that's when I know my baby and I will have a good time"

--*Surfin'* (B. Wilson/M. Love) The Beach Boys, 1962

In planning your first session, get your stuff organized in one place. Then, think about where and when to go. Choose the right conditions and the right beach, and avoid crowds of experienced surfers. Before you paddle out, warm up a bit on the beach and practice the basics of popping up. Think through popping up and the stance you will use to maintain your balance and turn your board. The more you practice these things on land, the more rewarding your experience will be in the water.

Your Stuff
It pays to be ready to go at a moment's notice. You might get the day off, or drive past an unexpected swell as the wind shifts to offshore, or get a call from a friend inviting you for a surf. To take advantage of that window, you need to have your stuff together. Along with your board, leash, and wetsuit (or trunks), Sean Tompson, a champion surfer from South Africa, recommends getting a surf bag to hold a few essential things. If you don't, you'll find yourself forgetting something or losing it in the sand.

Your surf bag should be of a style and material that can air out and dry (otherwise it will stay damp and start to smell). Several backpack manufacturers have "dry pouches" that are perfect for storing a wet wetsuit apart from your other gear. Other bags have mesh bottoms to allow your gear to dry out faster. Whatever the style, the bag will stay better organized if it has multiple pockets.

Your surf bag should contain things like:
1) A tide book
2) Some change for the parking meter
3) A magnetic key box (if you need to stash your car key)
4) Hard and soft wax in a wrapper or baggie (wax melts)
5) A UV-cure ding-repair kit
6) A wax comb
7) A fin key (to tighten loose fin screws)
8) An extra leash
9) Sunscreen
10) Antibiotic cream
11) Anti-friction lube
12) A towel for drying off and changing
13) Warm dry clothes (e.g., a hoodie or beanie)
14) An extra pair of flip-flops or sandals
15) A hairbrush
16) A snack
17) Bottled water

Sadly, at some beaches, you will have to worry about petty theft. The best theft deterrent is to lock your stuff in the car. But keep in mind that thieves might smash a window to grab your wallet. Put your stuff in the trunk instead of on the seat.

With your things securely in your car trunk, all you need to do is hold on to your car key. But stashing a key somewhere on the beach is not fool proof. My Brazilian friends still tease me about the time I hid my car keys under a coconut husk on the beach. While I was surfing, a community group raked the beach clean, along with the coconut and my keys, leaving me to hitchhike hike home in nothing but my board shorts. Fortunately, there are alternatives to coconuts. Many wetsuits and board shorts have a key pocket or loop of cord where you can securely keep a single key (if your shorts have a pocket with a strong Velcro seal, you can also keep a credit card or hotel key safely on you). Don't surf with a key that has an electric locking/unlocking mechanism, as seawater will damage it. Instead, you can use a magnetic box to hide a key somewhere on your car.

If you still want to bring a lot of stuff with you to the beach, you can either try to hide it or put it in a place where you can see it from the line up. Better yet, ask someone trustworthy on the beach if they will watch your things for you while you are surfing.

The Right Beach
Part of the challenge for the beginning surfer is finding conditions that are right for learning. While checking out potential spots, look for signs that advise against or prohibit surfing. For instance, polluted beaches are often marked as closed to swimmers and surfers, and others are posted with warnings due to dangerous currents or subsurface hazards. Lifeguards might post signs indicating the level of danger in the surf (often in colors indicating the level of hazard, like green, yellow, or red). Finally, some beaches exclude surfing from parts of the beach or times of day (e.g., with a black-ball sign) to minimize conflicts with swimmers. Respect signs indicating closures, even if you see other surfers in the water.

Online surf guides give a list of beaches in your area and often indicate whether a place is good for beginners. The ideal learner's spot has a sandy bottom, and gentle, but consistent waves. Once you get to the beach, ask a local to recommend the best part of the break for learning. If a spot seems right, take a close look at who is surfing. Shortboarders prefer punchier waves that are harder to learn on, and there is little point learning at a spot crowded with experienced surfers.

Forecasting
In the old days, we'd plan our sessions by listening to a weather service surf report. Here is an example of what we'd hear on our little cubic weather radios: "Most west-facing breaks early this morning were seeing sets running chest high and south-facing breaks were running knee to waist. Swell will increase as the day progresses.

Currently, periods on the incoming swell are running 15 seconds from 310° (with forerunners at 18 seconds), and there are also 6-10 second periods in the mix." An upgrade on those surf reports are surf cams that show the waves in real time and whether there is a crowd in the water. With a laptop or smart phone, you can now keep track of the waves anywhere in the world.

In addition to surf reports, there are now good online surf forecasts. Forecasters, by tracking wind speed, direction, and fetch over the ocean can estimate, days in advance, the size and timing of swells that will reach a coastline. These data come in easy-to-read maps and graphics. As long as you are not color blind, it is easy to plan your next session. All you need to do is get online and find a site that forecasts the beaches near you.

Convenience and predictability have a downside. Like the sirens of Greek mythology, forecasters lure surfers to the coast in droves by hyping each new swell on their website days before it arrives. There, surfers sit in packs and grumble about how crowded it has become ever since online forecasts. Unlike Odysseus, you don't have to plug your ears with beeswax (though that would help with the exostosis), just plan around the hype. If the forecast says the swell is peaking on Sunday, think about going surfing on Saturday or Monday. Or, if a swell is hyped, try to find a time when other surfers will be busy. Crowds are smallest in the early morning, and the wind tends to be calmer too. That's when you can sometimes score some quality empty waves.

You'll do even better if you become your own surf forecaster. Because surf forecasts are only a best guess, regular surfers keep track of how the weather forecast matches what they see at the beach. Regulars know that their break has its own response to the tide and wind direction. You can get your local beach wired too. First, get a head start by asking the locals. They will volunteer information like how great the surf was during the low tide when the wind was offshore (surfers love to tell you how much better it was before you got there). Then, try to keep a log about how the waves were during your visit and how this relates to the forecast, tide, and wind. Soon, your friends will be asking you for a surf report.

THE ESSENTIALS OF SURFING

Regular or Goofy?
Before you can practice popping up, you need to know which is your forward foot. Your front foot is not related to whether you are left or right-handed. You'll have to figure your footedness another way. If you already water ski, snowboard, or skateboard, you know which foot you put forward. If not, put your feet together, hands at the side, and have someone push you backwards. You will have to put a foot back to keep from falling. This is often your rear foot in surfing. Alternatively, have someone push you in the back. The foot you first put forward is your front. Another trick is to close your eyes and try to walk a straight line; you often veer toward the same side as your front foot. But don't do this near a cliff.

If you surf with your right foot back, you are called a "regular (or natural) footer." Regular probably refers to an early misconception that this was the most common stance. In contrast, a "goofy footer" surfs with the left foot back. This term might derive from Goofy's surf stance on an alaia in the cartoon short *Hawaiian Holiday* (Disney, 1937). Although both stances surf equally well, when learning, it is easier to surf frontside, which means facing the breaking wave. Right-breaking waves are easiest for regular footers, whereas goofy footers will find it easier to surf left-breaking waves.

Take a Lesson
You will save time, reduce frustration, and avoid learning bad habits if you take a surf lesson. A surf instructor will teach you to warm up, paddle out, and get through breaking waves. You'll learn how to place your weight, sit on your board and spin it around. But popping up to your feet will be the main goal of your first lesson. A group lesson is good for the first try, but a private lesson is worth investing for a second and third time. On top of surf lessons, watching other surfers catch waves, either at the beach or on the screen, will help you to visualize your upcoming surfing experience. But don't think you are going to surf like Kelly Slater on your first day.

Prepare Your Body
To surf well, you'll need your wits and a high energy level, so get a good night's sleep. Before heading to the beach, put on an extra layer of clothes to start off the session warm. You'll want these warm

clothes again later when you are chilled from your session. Remember to eat a good meal, but do it a few hours in advance. It's harder to surf on a full belly. And be sure to use the toilet before suiting up.

Some surfers like to stretch their arms, back, and legs before surfing, but trainers now suggest that you stretch following, not before, exercising. Instead of stretching, get your heartbeat up. A brisk walk or jog on the beach should be enough to break a mild sweat. Then, move the specific muscles that you are going to use while surfing. The most effective warm up for surfing is to pantomime paddling, popping up to your feet, twisting your trunk, and squatting. But don't overdo it. Save some energy for the water.

Practice on Land
Because popping up happens fast, doing it right requires muscle memory. This is the reflex you get from doing the same thing over and over. It's a way your body learns to move without thinking about it. For example, when you brush your teeth, or dry off with a towel, or do another repetitive motion thousands of times, you follow an unconscious pattern. That's muscle memory. Experienced surfers rely on the muscle memory they have gained from surfing thousands of waves. Popping to their feet becomes instinctual. They aren't even aware of the steps they take to do it.

The difficulty of getting the muscle memory for popping up is that you have few opportunities to practice in the water. On a good day, you might be able to try to stand up twenty times. But you'll need hundreds of times for your brain to start laying down dedicated neural synapses. For this reason, the secret to wiring your brain is to practice on land. You can start by drawing a line on the ground to represent the stringer of your board. Lie face down over the imaginary stringer that runs under your nose through your crotch. Pop up dozens of times on land and you will have a chance of getting it right in the water. Next, I will break the pop-up into four "ups". It might seem like over kill, but going through all the details shows how much needs to happen in a couple seconds.

THE ESSENTIALS OF SURFING

Popping up

The Coil-up

The coil-up prepares you to spring to your feet, like when a sprinter gets into the starting blocks before a race. You coil up just as the wave pushes your board forward. Imagine that you have taken your last paddle and are gliding under the power of the steepening wave. Now, with your body over the centerline, and your chest still on the board, place your palms flat (not fully grasping the rails) with each thumb under a nipple, as if preparing for a push up, but with your hands closer together. Your elbows will be sticking out to the side in a pose that some surf instructors call the "chicken wing". At the same time, place the ball of your rear foot on the board near the centerline. How far up from the tail you place your back foot depends on your size, the length of the board, and how much space you need to clear for your front leg. The more forward your back foot, the more space you will clear for the spring up.

Shortboarders can't plant a foot on the tail. They coil up from their back knee (this is one reason shorter boards are harder to surf). Some shortboarders also coil up by raising their feet above their butts so they can kick them down toward the board as they spring up.

The Push-up
When the nose of the board starts to point downward as the wave lifts the tail, it's time for the push-up. The push-up opens space for you to bring your front knee and foot forward under your chest during the spring-up. To push-up, elevate your trunk, but not your hips, as much as possible. As you raise your chest up, arch your neck and head up and back, looking forward, not down. This causes your center of gravity to shift back, which submerges the tail of your board and lifts the nose. Lifting the nose helps prevent your board from pearling (submerging, nose first). At the end of the push-up, some surfers will raise their butts high off their board. Because this position is unstable, don't hold it long. It's best to keep low.

The Spring-up
The hardest part of surfing is the spring-up. Springing up in one fast and simple movement (instead of crawling up) gets your front foot to the spot on the stringer that is between your hands. Spring-up when the board starts planing down the face of the wave. Wait too long, and you will find yourself at the bottom of the wave where it becomes much more difficult to get to your feet. Conversely, you will lose your momentum, and the wave will pass you by if you begin the spring-up too soon.

To spring up fast, push off of the toes of your back foot (which you planted on the deck near the tail during the coil-up) as you further lift your lower trunk off the deck. Then, swing your front knee under and across your chest. To end up in the correct stance, you must also twist your shoulders to face the side of the board. If you are a regular foot, you will be twisting your shoulders, and front knee to the right as you spring. If you are goofy foot, you will be twisting to the left. During the spring-up, your head and chest should stay high, and your butt should be lower than your head. Breaking the spring up into two steps can make it easier, so some surfers will take a small forward step with their back foot before springing up. The spring-up ends when you plant your front foot on the stringer where your chest started out. On a real wave, you won't be able to think through these steps. The best you'll manage is to try to get your forward foot to the spot between your nipples in one motion.

The Lever-up, a Word of Warning

An alternative to the spring-up sometimes taught in surf schools is the lever-up (or the Aussie sprint technique). This approach can help larger, and less coordinated people get to their feet. The lever-up further extends the coil-up by bringing the back foot up as far forward as possible along the centerline until the heel touches the butt. This causes the back knee to stick out over the rail of the board where it can be used as a lever point to help lift the trunk over the deck, making it easier for the front leg to pass under the chest when standing. This comes at a price. The lever-up initially puts the surfer's weight over the back foot, which can slow the board down. The lever up also takes more steps than the spring-up. Furthermore, the lever-up encourages an initial and secondary knee placement that stresses the knee joint, endangering several ligaments. Learn the spring-up if you can. It will pay off in the long run.

The Stand-up

If you did the spring-up right, your front foot will be planted on the stringer under your chest, pointed slightly forward. Your rear foot should also be on the stringer, but pointed perpendicular to the centerline of the board. You might need to slide your back foot forward to get it about shoulder width from your front foot (about where your knee started out). Too wide a stance and you won't be able to rotate your trunk to turn, too narrow a stance and you will be more likely to lose your balance and won't be able to pivot off your back foot when turning. At this point, many beginners cling to the board with their hands (often with their butts sticking up like a stink bug). However, you are more stable if you lift your hands from the board and raise your head and chest while keeping your butt low. You should be bent at the knees with the back straight and the arms outstretched. This stance will keep your center of gravity low and allow you to steer and control your board.

Riding across a wave requires balance through constant adjustment of your weight over the board. You can work this out on the beach with a simple technique. Build a solid mound of sand about a foot high and a foot in diameter and balance your board on the mound. Walk up on the board, from the tail, back leg first, and shuffle forward until you are balanced on the mound. Because the sand will compress under your weight, be sure that the mound is still high enough that your fins are clear of the sand (if not, add more sand). Next, get into your stance. Bend your knees and keep your back straight and look forward. Now, practice shifting your weight with your hips to raise the nose up and down. Next, try a turn by shifting your weight over your back foot a little, and swinging your forward shoulder across your body while leaning forward. This should swing the nose in a mock turn. Once you can do a frontside turn, try to turn backside. Practice turns until it feels second nature. But be gentle; standing on your board outside of the water can lead to dings and damage.

If it is more comfortable to pop up differently than I have described above, don't sweat it. Surfers have a variety of ways to get to their feet. As long as you pop up quick and don't plant your front knee before you plant your front foot, you are good to go.

Now you are ready to get in the water. You've chosen the right day, picked out an appropriate board and are wearing the right trunks or wetsuit. Furthermore, you have practiced popping to your feet and the stance you will use to trim and turn. All you need to do is get in the water and give it a try.

THE ESSENTIALS OF SURFING

Getting Ready Essentials
- *Choose an uncrowded beach.*
- *Check that the conditions are good for learning.*
- *Find your forward foot.*
- *Warm up.*
- *Place feet on the centerline.*
- *Point toes almost perpendicular to the centerline.*
- *Keep your knees bent.*
- *Look forward, not down.*
- *Use your outstretched arms for balance.*
- *Your front foot is your accelerator.*
- *Your back foot is your brake and steering.*
- *Practice popping up on the centerline.*
- *Practice balancing in your stance.*
- *Practice turning in your stance.*

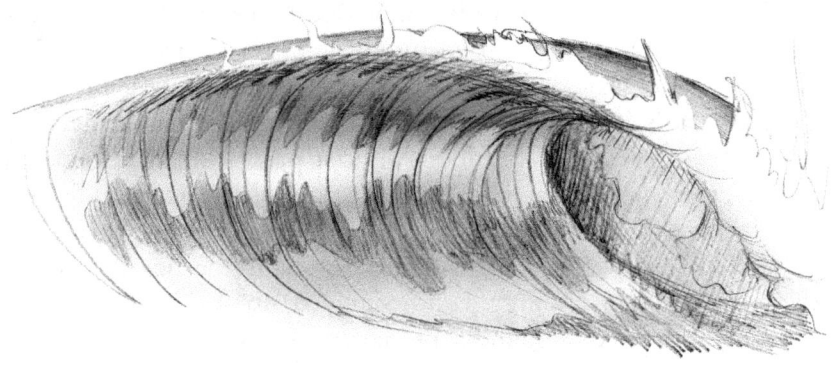

9. YOUR FIRST SESSION

Tyler (to Johnny Utah): "Both feet have to land on the board at the same time. That's it. That's it. You're surfing!"
--*Point Break* (20th Century Fox, 1991)

Surfers remember their first wave. Your first session will leave you bruised, sore, and chilled but, hopefully, triumphant, glowing, and proud. Success is simply a matter of finding a spot good for beginning, getting out to the waves, and waiting for a wave to paddle into. Choose a spot with small, spilling waves, and avoid large surf, particularly where there is a plunging beach break. With some luck, you'll be up on your feet and turning across the surface of the wave.

If you want a role model for catching a wave, watch a classy surfer like professional longboarder Joel Tudor. Here's Joel catching a wave. Sitting in the lineup he sees a glassy peak about head high. He slides back on his board, grabs the rising nose and spins it 180° to his left. He paddles to the peak in an arc as that the well rises behind him. His weight is forward, but his head is up and his back is arched so that the nose of his board does not pearl. After five quick strokes, the wave crests and his board starts to plane. To get speed for the take off, he lowers his head and bends his knees until his feet are lifted high off the board, shifting his weight forward. Two more hard strokes, and the board starts to fall down the face of the wave as Joel plants his palms on the deck of the board and pushes up his trunk, his weight on his thighs. He swings both feet underneath himself as the board falls. His right foot lands on the stringer, toes facing to his left. His back foot is under his left shoulder. Joel's fingers are still on the deck, his chest is almost touching his bent right knee, his head is up, and he's looking down the face of the wave. He straightens his back and stands, his knees are bent and already he has angled his board to the left, riding frontside. The first part of the wave is a bit fat so he cross steps to the nose to pick up some speed. He rides the nose a bit and then cross steps backwards to plant his left foot over the tail. With his weight over the tail, he pivots the board to do a cutback to his right. With the nose angled up, he banks off the approaching whitewater and turns again to his left. As the next section begins to close out in front of him, he steps far back on the tail, kicks the board up over the wave, and falls into the foam, letting the wave pass over his body.

Joel makes it look easy because he's done it thousands of times. As a result, he doesn't have to think about what he's doing. His mind is free to be creative and flowing. But you're a beginner; it's not going to seem that easy for you.

Catch the Whitewater
You might try postponing paddling into waves until after you practice catching the whitewater of breaking waves in the surf zone. Learning to pop up by catching the whitewater is best at shallow-sloping sandy beaches where the whitewater travels for several seconds before it hits dry sand. This gives you time to focus on learning to pop up before learning how to catch waves. It also gives you a sense of the thrill of catching a wave, which is a reward that will motivate you to learn how to catch waves on your own. It's as easy as sledding, but not as cold.

To catch the whitewater, walk out to where the water is knee to waist deep, between the breaking waves and the shore. Hold the board up until you see a good-sized wave break. Turn to shore and set the board down on the water while looking back over your shoulder at the oncoming wave. Just before the foam hits, jump forward onto the board. The white water will push you from behind all the way to the beach if all goes right. If the wave passes you by, you need to either move your weight a little forward, or push off harder. If you pearl, shift your weight back next time.

The first several times you catch the whitewater, steer the board on your stomach to learn how to place your weight. Practice pushing up on your board so you can see how adjusting your weight lifts and lowers the nose and changes your speed and control. But don't be tempted to surf on your knees, as this develops a bad habit. When you get to shallow water, slide your body back off the tail to let the wave pass you by before you crash into the sand.

Once you are comfortable catching the whitewater, practice popping up to your feet soon after the whitewater starts to move you forward (if you stand up before the wave begins to push you forward, the wave will pass you by). Keep in mind that it can be harder to pop up in the whitewater than on a cresting wave because your board does not drop down the face as you pop up to your feet. At first, you might fall over when you pop up. Take note of how you fall off. If you fall off to the side, you are either not on the centerline or you need to crouch down more to maintain your balance. If the board pearls when you stand, your weight is too far forward. If the wave passes you by, you are too far back. Despite making adjustments, some learners still have a hard time popping up in the white water and might need a bigger board or more practice on land.

If you have mastered catching the whitewater at a gently sloping beach, you can wade out to where the waves are breaking, and try the same thing on a cresting wave. Alternatively, you can have a friend push you into a cresting wave as you lie prone on the board. This will take you one step closer to paddling into a wave.

Paddling Out

To catch actual breaking waves (instead of broken waves) requires paddling through the surf zone to the lineup. Paddling sounds simple, but doing it right is not easy. Knowing where, when and how to paddle is the key to catching waves. If you are planning on going straight to tow-in surfing, skip this section.

You can save yourself a lot of trouble by planning where to paddle out. Choose a mellow part of the break with a sandy bottom away from where others are surfing. If the best spot is unclear, don't be shy to ask for help. Locals can tell you where the paddling channels are, if there are submerged rocks, and whether those rocks have sea urchins. I remember when eleven-time world champion Kelly Slater was in town on a big day at Campus Point. Kelly had never surfed there before, and he did not hesitate to ask the locals where to paddle out. But, if you ask for advice, be sure to mention that you are a beginner so as not to be confused with Kelly Slater.

If the waves are bigger than waist high, you'll need to time your paddle out for a lull in the waves. Wave consistency is greater when the wave period is short, and this makes it difficult to pick a time when no waves are breaking. But for longer period swells, the waves will come in sets. Paddling out during a set can be exhausting and leave you with little energy to catch waves. To avoid getting caught inside by a set, watch the waves for ten to twenty minutes until a set rolls through. Following this, the waves will often be small for 3-4 times as long as it took the set to break. This lull buys you time to get through the surf zone.

Once you've committed to a place and time, wade out to waist-deep water. When you get to waist-deep water and the impact zone looks clear of waves, point your board into the oncoming waves, lie own on it, adjust your position, and paddle. Paddling out is a race between you and the breaking waves. The less time you spend inside getting pounded by waves, the easier it will be to get out to your takeoff spot. Once you start, paddle hard.

There are several techniques for efficient paddling. The most important is adjusting your weight on the board. Shift your weight forward until the nose of the board is sitting only an inch above the surface of the water. Any more forward and you are in danger of pearling the nose of your board. If you are too far back, your board will push water as you paddle. When you find the right position, lower your face to the stringer and note where it is relative to the shaper's label. You can use this guide the next time you get on your board.

Now you can focus on your strokes. Some longboarders will paddle a butterfly-style stroke while on their knees, but this requires good balance to pull off. As a beginner, paddle with alternating strokes, like the free-style or crawl stroke in swimming. You can move fastest by stroking deep with cupped hands. Each hand should enter the water near the rail of the surfboard, pass deep under the rail, and emerge from the water next to the rail. Unlike in swimming, your body should not roll from side to side.

A sure sign of a beginner is a surfer that paddles with their legs splayed out to the side as they try to balance their board. Though this helps with balance, it creates drag that slows you down. Minimize drag by keeping your feet together and out of the water. You will soon learn to balance by shifting your weight with your knees and arms. You'll know you have it together when your board is planing fast with little effort.

To paddle your board in the correct direction, look where you are going by keeping your chin off the deck. To steer to the right, stroke with the right arm down under the board while stroking out shallow with the left arm. Do the opposite to steer left. Steering is harder with a longer board, requiring you to plan your course earlier.

No matter how good your timing or where you choose to paddle out, you will eventually face breaking waves bearing down on you. This is one of the most challenging and terrifying parts of learning to surf because you and the wave want to go opposite directions and, although you can't stop the wave, it can stop you. In all cases, your goal is to minimize conflict with the wave. Your first instinct will be to throw the board over the breaking wave or push your board to the side and dive. This instinct is bad form, ineffective, and dangerous.

This brings me to the number one tip for paddling out: always aim the nose of your board into the breaking waves. Waves provide resistance and you want to present the smallest area for them to push against. Going nose-sideways allows waves to hit your board broadside. Getting broadsided will stop your momentum, flip you over, and push your board back to shore like a Styrofoam cup. The nose-first rule also applies to wading out with your board. If you are holding your board sideways, a wave can flip the board up into your face. If you break the nose-first rule, you might break your nose.

How you get through the surf depends on the size of the waves and the type of board you have. Longboards paddle well, and if you give it your best effort, you can often pass over the wave before it breaks or angle around the breaking section. Pulling this off takes strength and experience judging breaking waves. If the wave crests before you get over it, the whitewater can lift the nose of the board, pushing you up and backwards. To reduce the impact of an oncoming wave, paddle hard into it, then push your torso up with your arms to sink the nose of the board under the foam while holding on tight to the rails with your weight forward over your hands. In this pose, the force of the whitewater will pass between you and the board, and you will soon be paddling forward again.

If the lip is starting to break on your head, you can duck to punch your board and body through the wave. Here, you also want to paddle hard before the impact. Then, with your weight over the nose, put your forehead on the deck of the board so that the passing wave rolls over your head onto your back. As soon as your head emerges from the water, paddle to prevent the wave from sucking you back over the falls. You can rest when you get out beyond the breaking waves.

Eskimo Roll
Longboarders use the Eskimo roll (or turn turtle) to get under large broken waves. The term Eskimo roll refers to flipping a kayak and getting it upright again. Honestly, I'm not sure why the phrase turning turtle is used in California (we don't have a lot of turtles). Executing an Eskimo roll is critical when the surf is big. Practice first on smaller waves.

Here is the process broken down into steps. When the oncoming whitewater is a board length away, grab the rails of the board at your chest, and quickly roll over with the board so that you are underwater hanging from the rails, pulling the nose underwater with a tight grip to prepare for impact. With the wave on top of you, straighten your arms to push your body deeper under the breaking wave, away from the turbulence. Once the wave passes over, pull with one arm and push with the other, while kicking hard, to flip the board over. Get back on your board as soon as possible, either by pulling yourself over the side, or by climbing onto the tail, aligning yourself with the stringer, and pulling yourself forward by the rails. If this seems hard, be glad you're not doing a real Eskimo roll in a kayak.

Duck Diving

Shortboarders duck dive under waves. Whether duck diving refers to ducking your head or to what ducks do, doesn't really matter. Duck diving is one of the more difficult surfing techniques, and it requires some practice. As the wave approaches, the shortboarder brings the rear knee up on the board or, to dive even deeper, the rear foot on the tail, while also extending the arms and leaning forward to push the nose under. (On a board that is too large to submerge, the surfer will need to either Eskimo roll, or submerge just one side of the nose.) The surfer's head should be underwater before the wave hits so the whitewater hits the surfer's butt, driving the board and surfer deeper under water. Once the whitewater passes over, the surfer gently presses the front knee (or back foot) into the board and pulls back on the nose to point the nose up. This will pop the nose out the back of the wave, where the surfer emerges ready to paddle.

Where to Sit

If you get tired from paddling out, you can rest a bit well beyond the breaking waves. This will give you a chance to catch your breath. But don't stay out there. To catch waves, you need to paddle back to the lineup.

One way to pick a spot from the beach is to look for other surfers who are catching waves. But remember your surfing etiquette. Don't paddle out close to another surfer if there are other, less crowded areas, particularly if that surfer has been waiting several minutes to catch a wave. You will irritate other surfers in the lineup if you paddle next to them, especially if you paddle around them and assume the right of way on the next wave that comes by. A good rule of thumb when paddling out into a pack of other surfers is to not contest a wave until the surfers that were there first have had a chance to paddle for a wave.

The Duck Dive

Intimidated beginners often sit too far outside of the lineup for fear of being caught inside. But getting caught inside is a risk you'll have to take to catch the smaller waves you can handle. Just be sure to keep an eye out for larger sets by scanning the horizon and watching the more experienced surfers who will paddle out when they see a set coming. If that happens, don't hesitate to paddle outside and get over the set waves (and get out of the way of the other surfers). Then, when the set passes, move back inside to catch some smaller waves.

Once you find a spot that is working for you, look to shore to get your bearings. Note the distance to the beach and find landmarks that indicate your lineup along the shore. Experienced surfers will often "line up" a series of near and far landmarks, like a tree, telephone pole, or a mountain peak, to triangulate their position.

To be able to see oncoming waves, always sit up on your board with the nose pointed out to sea. Don't lay down with your nose pointed to shore. As you sit, scoot back on the board until the nose sticks slightly out of the water; it is easier to pivot the board when your weight is over the tail. At first, sitting up will seem precarious. To keep your balance, put your hands in the water. You will figure out how to sit up without falling over in a few minutes. It's a bit like being drunk for the first time, but without the hangover.

Picking Your Wave
At first, you will paddle for waves that you have no chance of catching. You might try to catch waves that are already pitching or not breaking. Watching waves break and taking note of experienced surfers in the lineup will improve your timing and positioning.

If you see a wave peaking nearby, first look to see if other surfers with the right of way are paddling for it. If you think they will catch it, save your energy for the next wave. However, once you decide the wave is yours, don't hesitate to go for it.

Remember the golden rule to yield to surfers that are closer to the peak. Even if you have the right of way, let someone else have the wave if you don't think you can catch it. But if you are confident about your wave, give a shout to alert other surfers down the line that you are going for it. "I got it!" will be enough.

To help pivot the board toward the wave, you can grab the nose with your away hand and back paddle with the opposite arm. Alternatively, do a one or two-leg eggbeater kick, like water polo players do when they tread water. A clockwise beat will spin you to the left whereas a counter-clockwise beat will spin you to the right. After a spin toward the wave, you can lie prone and paddle to the peak.

Paddling Into a Wave

If you find yourself exhausted from paddling after waves that you don't catch, you are not getting your board to plane. Your board will only begin to plane down the face of a wave when it picks up enough speed to break the friction of the water. This requires paddling hard, and it's why surf instructors are always yelling "Paddle, paddle, paddle!" But it won't matter how hard you paddle if your weight is too far back; the nose of your board will push water and slow you down. You can adjust the nose by shifting your position on the board and lifting or lowering your head and chest. Shortboarders also point their toes back, or flutter kick, or lift their feet above the board to keep from dragging them like an anchor.

Paddling into a breaking wave is scary, like plunging headfirst off a small cliff. Normally, fear keeps us from taking bad risks, but hesitancy interferes with catching waves. Intimidated beginners miss waves because they shift their weight back, or paddle weakly, or sit too far out. If you find yourself backing off waves, remind yourself that the ocean is just water, and wiping out is better than missing a wave. Aim to take off on at least ten waves per session, whether you wipe out or not. Wiping out might be embarrassing, but you will get encouragement from surfer friends who will push you to go for it, if only because your wipeouts are entertaining.

Before you can pop up to your feet, the face of the wave needs to be steep enough for gravity to pull you and the board downward. For instance, when the face has less than a 45° slope, the wave will have a hard time pushing a surfer forward. Pop up now and the wave will pass you by. If the wave has lifted you, but is not pushing you forward, this is a sign to paddle harder so that you can help the board get into the wave as it steepens. However, at around 60°, the wave becomes unstable and is about to break, At this point, you will need to stop paddling and perhaps even shift your weight back to keep from pearling. Any steeper than 60° and it becomes hard to maintain control during take off. The sweet spot for taking off is when the wave is somewhere between a 45° and 60° slope. Be sure to have a protractor with you at all times.

Waves differ in how fast they go from 45° to breaking. For hollow waves formed at steep beaches, this can take less than a second; for crumbling waves formed at shallow beaches, a few seconds can lapse. Obviously, the more time the wave spends in the sweet spot, the easier it is to catch and the more forgiving it is for beginners. The sweet spot also depends on the type of board you are riding. Longboards can take off on shallower slopes; shortboards can negotiate steeper peaks, whereas fish can take off on a wide range of slopes.

The slope of the wave determines the best angle for taking off. For instance, on a gentle wave, surfers usually point the nose straight at shore. However, some longboarders will fade their takeoff into the curl, setting up a dramatic 180° turn on the face once they get to their feet. On a steep wave, the takeoff must be angled away from the curl. Angling the takeoff on a steep wave helps avoid pearling and can give you a head start down the line, which is helpful if the waves are closing out or sectioning or if you are behind the peak when you take off. But angling the takeoff also requires better balance and control, so it is harder for beginners to master – yet another reason to stick to gently sloping beaches.

As your board picks up speed and the wave begins to rise behind you, the nose of a longboard can pearl below the surface. If it does, you can kiss your wave goodbye. A successful take off is a compromise between stalling and not pearling. Before the nose pearls, shift your weight back. Usually, you won't need to slide your whole body toward the tail, just arch your back to shift your center of balance back. That'll pull your nose up, and keep you planing. But don't over correct; too much weight on the tail and you will stall, and the wave will leave you behind.

Popping Up
Now comes the critical part – getting to your feet. As you start to plane, the wave is pushing you forward on your board. You've moved from the coil-up to the push-up, looking down from the crest of the wave to the water below. Part of your brain is telling you this is a bad idea, whereas another part is telling you to stand up (these are the same parts of your brain that tell you to brush your teeth, and get a tattoo, respectively). You only have half a second to go from lying down to standing up, so listen to the get-a-tattoo side of your brain, and do the spring-up in a single step like you practiced on the beach. Without hesitating, you need to push the board down the face of the wave with your arms while lifting your front foot and placing it on the centerline under your chest, with your back foot a step and a half behind, followed by letting go of the board with your hands as you stand up. If you have done this a many times on land, it will come easier than trying to sort it out for the first time on a moving wave.

With popping up, timing is everything. Beginners often get anxious and try to stand too early. If you try to get to your feet before you start planing, your weight will be shifted back too soon, causing you to stall. Once the board loses its momentum, the wave will pass you by. If you continue to stall during takeoff attempts, keep prone on the board with your weight forward, and wait until the wave is really pushing you down the face. But don't wait long or you will take the drop on your belly and be too fast and out of control to get to your feet. Only practice will help you time your pop up to the breaking wave.

Getting into the Face
At first, when you pop up, your ride will be short, slow, and mired in the whitewater. Instead, you want to race parallel to shore in front of the breaking section on the open face of the wave. Surfing along the unbroken face harvests the forward speed of the swell and the lateral speed of the curl. Surfers can cruise along at more than 10 miles per hour on a decent wave. On steep faces of large waves, a surfer's speed can exceed 30 miles per hour.

THE ESSENTIALS OF SURFING

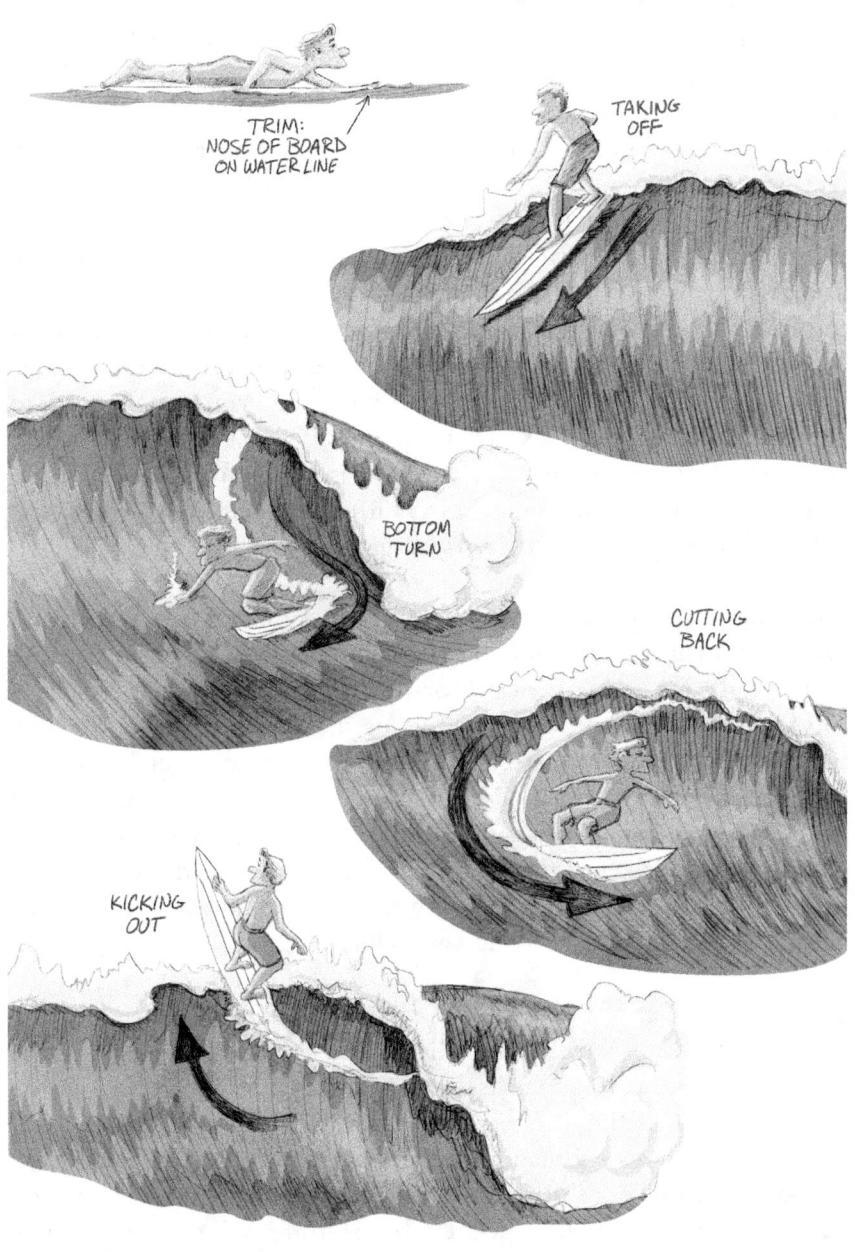

Basic Surfing Maneuvers

To surf the unbroken face of a steep wave, you need to turn your board the direction the wave is breaking. As mentioned earlier, a good head start is to angle your takeoff so that you are already pointed away from the curl when you pop up. Alternatively, you can drop in straight toward shore and then turn your board into the open face. On a mellow wave, leaning on your toes or heels (depending on whether you are turning frontside or backside) will result in a gradual turn. But a gradual turn often won't cut it. To get back into the pocket, you usually need to make a bottom turn. Carving a bottom turn on a shortboard first requires shifting your weight to your back foot to help the board pivot. On a longboard, because your normal stance does not place your feet over the tail, you might need to shuffle a step or two back. Then, with your feet set, look to where you want to go and point your forward hand and chest that way. This will help to rotate your trunk for the turn. At the end of the turn, you will need move your weight forward again to regain speed.

Speed and turning depend on weight distribution and foot placement. Once on their feet, beginners often submerge their nose because their weight is too far forward, or they stall because their weight is too far back. Think of the front foot as the accelerator and the back foot as the brake and steering wheel. Too much weight on the accelerator and you crash. Too much weight on the brake and you never get anywhere. Constant adjustment of your weight from one foot to the other keeps the board moving along with the wave while maintaining the nose above the surface of the water. It's just like driving through traffic on your way to the beach.

For the best ride, you will want to stay right in front of the breaking lip in the pocket of the wave. The pocket is the fastest part of the wave and where you will have the most fun. Once in the pocket, the surfer can stay at the steepest part of the wave face by maintaining trim. Trim requires subtle adjustments in pressure on the front foot, so that the board does not ride too high or too low on the face. You can stay deeper in the pocket by shifting your weight back. Alternatively, if you outrun the pocket, you can execute a cutback turn to angle the board back down the face, letting the curl catch up to you before doing a bottom turn and getting into trim again. Whatever you do, don't hop up and down on your board to keep it moving. Hopping looks awkward and does not help you stay in the pocket. Your surfboard is not a pogo stick.

The best advice I ever heard about surfing in the pocket is from Sean Tompson whose mantra is, "hard off the bottom, hard off the top." It describes a style of surfing based on sharp top and bottom turns. This helps the surfer work the full vertical range of the pocket and maintain the speed needed to pull off advanced moves. In surfing, as in life, one good turn deserves another.

Ending Your Ride

At some point, every ride ends. In the beginning, the end of your ride will often come when you wipe out. Wiping out is hard to plan, but fall behind your board to avoid hitting it, and also avoid diving head first toward the bottom. If the wave is small, just fall backwards into the whitewater. The wave will then push your body upright and you can retrieve your board. If the wave is large, try to hit the water in front of the wave with your butt or feet, legs bent, and sink below the whitewater. Then, as the broken wave is passing over you, spread your arms to maintain your balance, twist until you are facing away from shore, and reach for the bottom with your hands and feet. You can then push off the bottom for the surface as the turbulence subsides. When surfacing from a wipeout, be sure to lead with your hands to avoid coming face first into your board.

When a wave closes out, you have nowhere to go. You can be like Joel Tudor and lean back while doing a bottom turn to shoot the board up and over the wave. If you can't send the board over the wave, straighten out and head toward shore while steering around other people in the water. After straightening out, you can step or kneel back to sink the tail under the whitewater as you drag your front foot in the water, holding onto your board until the wave passes.

A good ride is like writing a clean sentence, and a good sentence ends with proper punctuation. Unfortunately, for most beginners, that punctuation is a question mark. For instance, a common and ungainly beginner's ending is to jump off the board feet first when the wave peters out. This not only looks awkward, it can be dangerous in shallow water. Another clear sign of a beginner is to sink the tail, fall backwards, and let the board shoot randomly into the air. Either way, the beginner has lost control of their board, putting others at risk. A safer and more practical end to a ride involves kicking out. This is like using a period in a sentence: simple, functional, and inconspicuous. To kick out, a surfer must first anticipate that the wave is ending, then steer the board over the lip of the wave before the wave closes out. At the end of the kick out, the nose should be pointed up and the board will sink tail first into the water as it loses speed. At this stage, the surfer can grab the nose and lean forward onto the board ready to paddle out. Once the surfer becomes more experienced in plunging waves, an alternative is to do a top turn and ride down with the crashing lip. This showy end captures the full power of the wave, like an exclamation point.

Calling it Quits

After an hour or two, most beginners tire out. Don't wait until you are so cold or exhausted that you have lost your coordination. It's better to end on a good note and head in. Ideally, you want to end your session by surfing back to the beach. Riding in is a lot less work than paddling in and is the honorable way for a surfer to end a session. But it always seems like the waves stop coming when you decide to take the next one in. When you are ready, paddle inside a little where the waves are more consistent and catch the next available wave.

Along rocky coasts, look for a break in the rocks where you can paddle in safely. Take care not to run your board into submerged rocks. Once the water is waist to knee deep, slide off your board and walk. Before walking in, remove your leash to keep it from snagging, watch the shore break behind you, and take care when stepping on hard or slippery surfaces. The worst ending to a surf session is to get hurt coming in.

When I had been surfing a couple years, I paddled out on a big day at Rincon that was beyond my skill level. I was not that familiar with the break, and after paddling out, I was too tired to think how I was getting back to the beach. A few waves later, I got caught inside, and the long-shore current took me past the sandy beach to the rocky revetment next to the highway. There, through the head-high shore break, I had to scramble up the boulders onto the road shoulder, where I'm sure I seemed out of place to passing motorists. I've been careful to plan my exit ever since.

If your first session resulted in your first wave, congratulate yourself. Getting to this point took putting together several new and complicated steps. And there will be plenty of better waves should you choose to stick with the sport. Remember the moment and savor it – there will never be another first wave.

Surfing Essentials

- *Don't put the board sideways between you and a wave.*
- *Choose a calm time and place to paddle out.*
- *Point your nose into the wave.*
- *Find the sweet spot on the board for planing.*
- *Push over small broken waves.*
- *Push under small oncoming waves.*
- *Eskimo roll or duck dive under large broken waves.*
- *Paddle with your head up, without rocking, and with deep strokes.*
- *Paddle hard, rest later.*
- *Avoid other surfers while paddling.*
- *Sit and wait for a wave away from others.*
- *Get your bearings.*
- *Pivot toward the peak.*
- *Yield to surfers with right of way.*
- *Paddle hard as the wave begins to lift you.*
- *Adjust your weight to maintain speed, but not pearl.*
- *Pop up in one motion.*
- *Get into your stance.*
- *Turn into the face of the wave.*
- *Maintain trim by shifting your hips.*
- *Hard off the bottom, hard off the top.*
- *Exit the wave safely and with style.*
- *Paddle back out for more waves.*
- *Quit before you are cold and exhausted.*

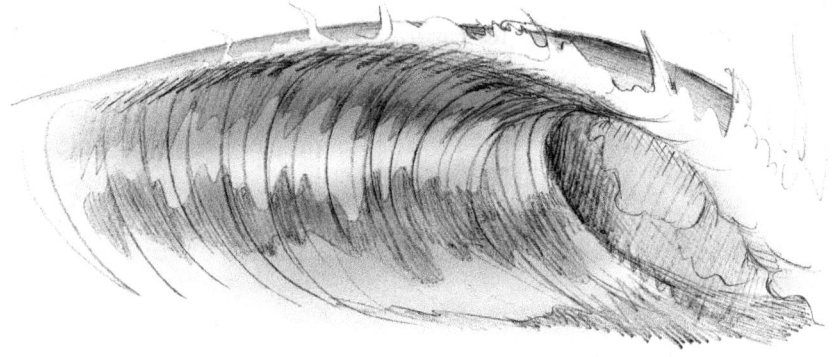

10. BEYOND BEGINNING

"These men were so excited about surfing that we felt sure, after we left, they'd shape their own surfboard from some jungle tree and are probably out there surfing right now."
--Bruce Brown, in *The Endless Summer* (Image Entertainment, 1976)

Once you have mastered paddling out, popping up, and finishing a ride, you are no longer a beginner. To get to this point takes considerable effort, practice, and adherence to the essentials of surfing. But that's only the beginning. To get better, you'll need to find good waves, surf a lot, and make your surf sessions fun. It can take a surfer years to reach their potential. Surfers differ in athletic skill and natural talents. Yours will improve fastest if, when you get comfortable, you push your boundaries by paddling out into more powerful surf, and by moving on to higher performance surfboards. When not in the water, skateboard or do other balance sports and stay in shape. Observe how other surfers interact and get along. Watch other surfers and develop your own style. Then, be sure to get a lot of waves. Before you know it, you will be giving beginners a few tips.

Surfing well requires a driving passion. Passionate surfers are committed to getting in the water. They paddle hard for waves, stay focused, and are confident in their abilities. The very best surfers set performance goals and work on them until they can add another skill to their repertoire.

Staying Fit

You will find it a lot easier to improve your surfing if you stay fit. A young surfer once asked for training advice from surfing legend Sean Tompson. Sean replied, correctly, that the best training for surfing was surfing. Unfortunately, most surfers can't surf as many hours as it would take to get all the exercise they need. Even the pros have training programs to stay in top form. When you can't get to the beach, think of other things to do instead of surfing the Internet.

The lungs are the most important part of the body for a surfer to keep healthy. Don't compromise them by smoking. I was telling an old surfing friend of mine about a big swell due to arrive. He frowned as he remarked that he wished he could get back into surfing, but he was a smoker now and couldn't quit. He felt too out of shape to surf and had sold his boards.

Surfing is also more difficult if you are overweight. The heavier you are, the less your board will float. This will increase drag in the water, making it more difficult to paddle. It will also take more effort to lift your mass when you pop up. That is not to say that being heavy keeps you from surfing. Plenty of big surfers rip. It's just more challenging.

Following your lungs and weight, take care of your aerobic capacity and your paddling strength. Paddling for waves requires a good mix of fast-twitch and slow-twitch muscle fibers in your back, arms, and chest. The best way to develop these muscles, outside of paddling a surfboard, is swimming. Other aerobic exercises, like running and biking, will help keep you trim and in shape, but they won't improve your paddling power like swimming will.

Weightlifting can help improve your paddling power, as long as you focus on light weights and multiple repetitions (for instance, weight that you can lift between 10 and 20 repetitions). In the weight room, do exercises that work your back, shoulders, triceps, and chest. But don't over do it; bulking up favors fast-twitch muscle fibers that, by themselves, are not suited for paddling. Body builders are better off displaying their muscles on the beach than using them in the waves.

Advanced surfers must be agile. Competitive sports, martial arts, and even dancing, will help improve the timing and coordination that surfing demands. Advanced surfers are also flexible. Stretch after exercising (including surfing), or use yoga as a way to stay limber and build core strength.

Surfing requires balance. Rolling balance boards (caution advised) are marketed to surfers and slack lining (walking a strap tied between two trees) helps develop poise and balance. A similar balance sport to surfing is snowboarding, and many surfers also snowboard. Whenever I snowboard, I imagine what it would be like to surf a ten minute wave and then take a chairlift back out to the break. Then I eat it on a patch of ice, get snow down my pants, and remember how much I prefer surfing. Of all the sports, surfing is most similar to skateboarding, and many skateboarding tricks translate directly into modern surfing tricks. When it's flat, go skateboarding. Just be careful. Concrete is harder than water.

Getting Along

You will see that surfers interact differently in the water than they do on land. In particular, some surfers become territorial in the water and are less open to small talk or chatting with strangers. But surfing is more fun if you can break the ice. Here are some ideas for how to start a conversation in the lineup. Ask the surfer next to you something simple, like how the surf was yesterday, or what time it is, or what the tide is doing. If you see someone get a nice wave, let him or her know. Secretly, all surfers want to impress their peers and you can make a friend by validating that need. Most importantly, apologize for getting in someone's way before that person snarls at you. On the other hand, it's bad form to talk smack in the line up or celebrate your accomplishments. Asking your buddies if they saw your most recent barrel or snappy turn confirms to the rest of the crowd that you are insecure. Work that out with your therapist instead.

Other surfers might not be pleased to share a wave with you, but on the beach, we'll share stories with you about waves, surf spots, and surfing. It helps the conversation if you know whom you are talking with. Ask the regulars about how the break works, ask the locals about the neighborhood, and ask the elders about the old days. In time, you'll build a group of surfing acquaintances and maybe even some new friends.

At some point, you will no longer be the newest surfer in the water. You will be able to catch more and more of the waves you want and establish confidence in the lineup. As you get better, keep in mind what it was like to learn. Recall the hours you spent watching others get waves while you flailed. So be friendly to beginners. Just because you can paddle around less experienced surfers and take all the good waves, remember that the happiest surfers are the ones that share and have fun in the water. No one likes a wave hog, so give a good wave away now and then. Smile in the line up and encourage friends and strangers alike.

Developing a style

You can learn to avoid the awkward surfing style that plagues most beginners. As stated above, don't bend at the waist; bend at the knees. Don't hop up and down on your board to try to make it go faster; shift or slide your weight forward instead. Don't flail your arms like a helicopter; point your upper body where you want to go and turn with your hips. Don't go in a straight line; go hard off the bottom, hard off the top. Don't fall off your board when the wave is over; focus on ending your ride well. Don't wear socks with your sandals; pair your un-tucked aloha shirt with flip flops.

Each surfer has his or her own style. Some are fluid, others strong. Some attack the wave, others glide with it. Watching surf films and the local surfers in your line up will expose you to a range of styles, help you elevate your style, and push you to take off on waves that would otherwise intimidate you. You will develop a style that fits your personality and your surfboard. For instance, a high-energy, aggressive style works best on a shortboard, whereas a longboard is better suited for classic trimming and gliding.

Get more waves

You can't improve unless you catch waves. But most learners get few waves due to ignorance and fear. Having read *Essentials of Surfing*, you are no longer ignorant and you can choose the best days to get waves.

You'll get more waves if you avoid these ten problems:

1. Choosing too short a board
2. Choosing unsuitable conditions
3. Sitting too far out
4. Sitting away from the peak
5. Sitting where it's too crowded
6. Shifting your weight too far back
7. Not paddling hard enough
8. Backing off due to fear
9. Waiting too long to pop up
10. Popping up too early

I'm grateful that surfing became a key part of my life after I watched Gerry Lopez win at Pipeline. What I've learned along the way is in *The Essentials of Surfing*. I hope reading it sets you on your own surfing adventure.

Essentials of Getting Better
- *Watch other surfers.*
- *Stay in good shape.*
- *Make friends.*
- *Be nice to beginners.*
- *Get more waves.*

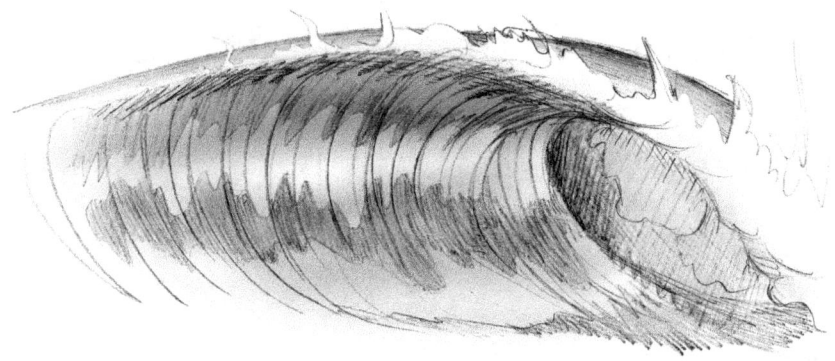

11. NOW GO SURFING

"Let's go surfin' now. Everybody's learnin' how."
--*Surfin'* (B. Wilson/M. Love) The Beach Boys, 1962

You now know the essentials of surfing. You understand waves, and know your way around a surfboard and a wetsuit. You'll learn faster, avoid bad habitats, and be less likely to injure yourself. You'll avoid conflicts with other surfers, you can walk into a surf shop with confidence, and you can talk to other surfers on the beach. If you excel, you can move onto advanced skills, such as pulling aerials, riding big waves, or tube riding.

How long can you surf? Kelly Slater once said "It's like the mafia. Once you're in – you're in. There's no getting out." But that's Slater. Like radioactive isotopes, surfers have a half-life. I'd guess that if you start with a hundred young surfers, 50 will still be surfing regularly after their first job, 25 after marriage, 12 after the first child, and so on. A lifetime of surfing requires living near consistent surf and having the free time to get in the water several times a month, if not several times a week. For instance, consider this useful surfing pun: "Sorry, I can't clean out the garage, I have a board meeting." Serious surfers build a life style around surfing by choosing their geography and adopting flexible or minimal work hours. But whether you surf for a lifetime or just a summer, learning to surf will expand your mind and link you with a select tribe of surfers around the world.

ABOUT THE AUTHOR AND ILLUSTRATOR

Professor Kevin Lafferty learned to surf in the 70's on a beater board in southern California and now lives at his home break in Goleta. He is a marine biologist and has traveled the world doing research, usually with surfboard in tow. He is the faculty adviser to the perennial national champion UC Santa Barbara surf team. As a hobby, he shapes and rides agave and redwood surfboards.

JR Johnson is a life-long California surfer. He holds a BFA in illustration, and has been a freelance cartoonist and illustrator since the 90's. His cartoons and illustrations appear in newspapers, magazines, and advertising nationally. Nowadays he surfs near his home in Orange County.

GLOSSARY

A-frame: a wave that peaks sharply, allowing a surfer to go either left or right.
Aerial: a maneuver where the surfer flies from the wave into the air while still on the surfboard.
Alaia: a simple surfboard of ancient Hawaiian design.
Amplitude: the height of a swell from trough to crest.
Backside/backhand: surfing with your back to the wave. For a goofy footer, going right is backside. For a regular footer, going left is backside.
Backwash: when a broken wave reflects back from the shore into incoming waves.
Bail: to jump off your board (usually to minimize the impact of a wipeout or collision).
Barrel: synonym for tube.
Bells Beach: a right point break outside of Melbourne, Australia.
Black ball: a sign or flag on the beach in California indicating that surfing is not permitted.
Black's Beach: a beach break near a submarine canyon in San Diego County, California.
Blown out: when strong wind degrades the waves, making it difficult to surf.
Board shorts: (Surf trunks) long, light shorts designed for surfing.
Bodyboard: a square, foam board ridden prone, or on one knee.
Bottom turn: turning into the face from the bottom of the wave.
Break: (1) when the crest of a wave collapses (2) a named location where surfing occurs.
Breakwater: a line of rocks installed to take the force of breaking waves, such as at a harbor mouth.
Buoyancy: referring to how well a material floats.
Butterfly stroke: when both arms come forward at the same time.
Captain James Cook: British explorer and first European to visit the Hawaiian Islands.
Centerline: an imaginary line from the nose to the tail down the middle of the board (usually aligned with the stringer).
Center of gravity: the midpoint of mass of a crouching surfer or of a surfboard.
Choppy: when small waves occur on the surface of the water.
Closeout: when the wave breaks in front of a surfer as the surfer planes across the face of the wave.

Cloth: fiberglass woven into a fabric.
Conditioning: exercising to get in shape.
Coral: a group of invertebrates (coelenterates) related to anemones that form skeletons of calcium carbonate, which, in aggregate, can make reefs.
Crest: the top of a swell.
Cresting: the swell just before it breaks.
Critical: a description of the steep section of an unbroken wave just before breaking.
Crossed up: when swells from different directions hit the shore at the same time. E.g., a wind swell from the west can cross up a ground swell from the south.
Cross step: moving sideways to the front or rear of a surfboard by crossing one foot ahead of the other.
Crowd: the number of surfers in the water.
Curl: the shape the pitching lip of the wave makes as it breaks (in cross section).
Current: the movement of water, usually due to tide or wind.
Cutback: to suddenly reverse direction and head back toward the curl.
Dawn Patrol: going surfing at sunrise.
Deck: the part of the surfboard you lie on.
Deck patch: an extra layer of fiberglass that makes the deck more durable.
Delamination: when the glass layer separates from the foam of the surfboard.
Ding: any kind of break in the glass layer of the board.
Drag: friction that slows movement.
Drop in on: taking off in front of a surfer that is already to their feet.
Duck dive: passing under a wave by pushing the board and body under.
Eggbeater: a swimming kick involving moving the foot in a circle.
Eskimo roll (Turn Turtle): to pass under a wave by rolling the board over.
Epoxy: a type of plastic resin, mixed with hardener, used to coat fiberglass cloth and form the hard shell of a surfboard.
Exotosis (Surfer's ear): bony growths that constrict the ear canal.
Face: the unbroken front of a wave in the process of breaking.
Fetch: the distance of ocean over which a storm blows.
Fiberglass: glass and plastic stretched into long fibers.
Fin: the part of the surfboard set under the tail of the board that help keeps the board moving straight.
Fish: a short, wide, and thick surfboard, so named because most have forked tails.
Flat: when the swell is too small to surf.
Flex: the amount the deck of a surfboard bends as you stand on it (a little flex is ideal).

Foam: (1) the light core of a surfboard, (2) a mix of air and water generated by a breaking wave.
Foam ball: A mass of foam that can form in the curl of a tubing wave.
Forecasting: predicting surf using knowledge of weather, tide, and characteristics of the beach.
Frontside: surfing with your face to the wave. For a goofy foot, going left is frontside.
Funboard: a medium length (7-9'), wide, surfboard with a rounded nose.
Glassy: smooth ocean conditions with no chop.
Goofy foot: a surfing stance with the right foot forward.
Grinding: when a long section of a wave breaks with great force from top to bottom.
Groin: a line of large rocks put into the surf zone to reduce beach erosion.
Grom: a young surfer (e.g., <16 years).
Gun: a board shaped for big waves with a pointed nose and tail.
Headland: a high point of land that sticks out from shoreline.
Heaving: when a wave surges forward with great force.
Heavy: describing a large and powerful wave.
Hold down: when a breaking wave holds a surfer under water.
Hollow: a wave that breaks as a cylinder.
Hull: a surfboard characterized by a v-shaped bottom.
Huntington Beach: a beach break in Orange County, California.
Inside: The area of water between a breaking wave and the shore.
Interval: the time, in seconds, (or Period) it takes two peaks of a swell to pass the same point.
Jack up: when a swell crests rapidly into a breaking wave.
Jeffrey's Bay: a right point break in South Africa.
Jellyfish: a group of invertebrates (coelenterates) related to anemones that swim in the ocean. Some float on the water. They vary in the strength of their sting.
Jetty: a long line of rocks perpendicular to the shoreline to stabilize a river mouth or bay entrance.
Kelp bed: a large mass of brown algae that floats on the surface.
Kick out: to exit the wave by putting weight on the tail and turning over the lip of the wave to the back of the wave.
Kook: an inexperienced surfer that makes a fool of themselves.
Leash: a cord that connects a surfer to the surfboard.
Leash cuff: the portion of the leash that wraps around the ankle.
Leash plug: a small cup embedded in the part of the surfboard where the leash attaches.
Leash webbing: a part of the leash made of fabric, attached near where the leash connects to the board (designed to increase the surface area of the leash where it contacts the board).

Line: an imaginary line that you make as you surf along the wave face.
Lineup: the location where surfers sit to wait for breaking waves.
Lip: the most forward part of the curl of a wave.
Local: a surfer that lives near the break (not needing to drive to get there).
Longboard: a board nine feet or longer with a rounded nose.
Long-shore current: a current that runs parallel to shore in the surf zone.
Lull: a period between sets when the waves are small.
Macking: a large swell when it nearing its peak size.
Moss Landing: a beach break near an underwater canyon in Monterrey County, California.
Mushy: waves that break gradually.
Neoprene: a stretchy, rubbery material that insulates when wet.
Nose: the front tip of a surfboard.
Offshore wind: wind that blows from land to sea.
Onshore wind: wind that blows from sea to land.
Over the falls: wiping out by coming down with the curl.
Outside: beyond the breaking waves.
Paddle: (1) to propel your board forward with your arms. (2) the device used to propel a stand-up paddleboard
Peak: the highest point of a breaking wave, where the wave breaks first.
Peaky: when the waves are breaking with well-defined peaks.
Peeling: a wave that breaks smoothly along its open face.
Period: the time, in seconds, (or Amplitude) it takes two peaks of a swell to pass the same point.
Pitched: when a surfer is pushed forward off the wave by the breaking lip.
Pitching: a wave with a lip that is thrown forward.
Pivot: to turn the nose of the board with the surfer's weight over on the tail.
Planing: when the board moves fast enough that it gains lift, reducing drag.
Plunging wave: a wave that breaks quickly. This is caused by a sloping bottom. Plunging waves are hard to learn on, but experienced surfers seek their energy.
Pocket: the section of the breaking wave closest to the curl.
Point break: a type of wave, usually formed by a headland, where the wave breaks predictably in a long wall.
Point Mugu: an "off-limits" beach break near an underwater canyon on a naval base in Ventura County, California.
Polyurethane: the most common type of plastic resin, mixed with hardener, used to coat the fiberglass cloth and form the hard shell of a surfboard.
Popping up: getting from the prone position to your feet in one motion.
Pressure ding: a depression in the surface of the board (often caused by a knee or heel) that does not let in water.

Prone: lying face down.
Punta de Lobos: a left point break near Santiago, Chile.
Pearl: when the nose of the board goes under water, stopping motion.
Rag dolled: getting caught underwater in the turbulent section of the wave so that you have no control of your position.
Rail: the edge of a surfboard.
Rail saver: a wide strap that connects the leash to the leash plug.
Rashguard: a thin, stretchy shirt worn while surfing.
Reef pass: a deep cut through a coral reef that allows water to enter a lagoon.
Reform: a wave that breaks on a reef or bar then stops breaking as it enters deep water, only to break again in shallow water.
Regular foot: a surfing stance with the left foot forward
Right of way: indicating the surfer who has priority for surfing a wave (i.e., who is sitting closest to the peak).
Rincon: a right point break in Santa Barbara County, California.
Rip: to surf well.
Rip tide: a current caused by breaking waves that moves offshore from the beach.
Rocker: the curve of a surfboard when looking at the rails from the side of the board.
Rolled: getting caught underwater in the turbulent section of the wave so that you have no control of your position.
Rotator cuff: Tendons and muscles surrounding the shoulder socket.
S glass: a type of weave for surfboard cloth.
Sand bar: a shallow, and usually temporary, underwater formation of sand that can cause a wave to peak.
Score: to get good waves.
Sea lion: a pinniped (type of marine mammal) with exterior ears.
Sea urchin: an herbivorous invertebrate with a spherical body and sharp spines.
Seal: a pinniped (type of marine mammal) with interior ears.
Seawall: a hard structure made to protect coastal property from erosion.
Section: a segment of the face of a breaking wave.
Session: the time between paddling out and paddling in.
Set: two or more waves together in time.
Shore break: the waves that break on or near the shore.
Shortboard: a small, high performance surfboard, usually similar in length as the rider is tall, with a narrower profile than a fish.
Shorty (Springsuit): a wetsuit with short legs and arms.
Shoulder: the unbroken face of a breaking wave.
Shred: to surf well.
Single fin: any board with one fin.

Skeg: the center fin of a longboard.
Sketchy: vernacular for when conditions seem dangerous.
Skimboard: a flat board without fins used for sliding across wet sand after a wave retreats.
Slacklining: balancing on a strap strung between two trees or posts.
Snake: to paddle around another surfer to get priority position for an approaching wave.
Softboard: a surfboard made of soft, flexible foam.
Spin: to turn around while sitting on the board to face the shore before paddling into a wave.
Spilling wave: a wave that breaks slowly, usually over a flat bottom. This gives a beginning surfer ample time to get to their feet, but provides little power for a shortboarder.
Spit: a long, shallow sand bar where waves break.
Spitting: when foam is exhaled out of a collapsing tube.
Springsuit (Shorty): a wetsuit with short legs and arms.
Stance: the way a surfer stands on a surfboard.
Stand-up paddleboard (SUP): a large, thick surfboard powered by a paddle while standing up.
Steepness: the slope of the face of the wave.
Stick: slang for surfboard.
Stoked: to be thrilled.
Storm drain: a location where run off is channeled to the ocean.
Stroke: a single paddle.
Suited up: to get into a wetsuit.
Sucked out: a wave that becomes hollow as it hits shallow water.
Superbank: a right point break on the Gold Coast of Australia formed by a sand dredge.
Surf racks: special roof racks for transporting surfboards on cars.
Surf trunks (Board shorts): shorts specifically designed for surfing.
Surf zone: the area of the ocean where the waves are breaking.
Surfer's ear (Exotosis): bony growths that constrict the ear canal.
Surging wave: a wave that breaks suddenly on the beach, caused by a steep bottom and difficult or impossible to surf.
Sweeper: a derogatory name for a stand-up paddleboarder.
Sweet spot: (1) a position on the board where foot placement leads to efficient planing and turning. (2) a part of the pocket of the wave that gives a surfer the greatest speed.
Swell: unbroken waves as they move toward the coast.
Swell height: the size of the wave from the trough to the peak.
Swell window: range of directions from which waves can reach a particular surf spot.
Takeoff: the process of paddling into a wave and popping up.

Teahupo'o: a reef pass on the island of Papeete in French Polynesia.
Thickness: the measurement of a surfboard in cross section at the stringer.
Thumping: the sound of a crashing lip. OR pertaining to big surf.
Tide: a local change in the water level of the ocean due to the gravitational pull of the sun and moon.
Top turn: a downward turn executed at or near the lip of the wave.
Traction pad: a piece of textured foam stuck to the deck of a board (usually at the tail) to increase traction.
Trough: the bottom of a swell.
Trunks: shorts specially designed for surfing.
Trunk it: to surf wearing only trunks.
Tsunami: a wave created by an earthquake or underwater avalanche.
Tube: the open space formed by the curl of a hollow, breaking wave.
Turn turtle (Eskimo roll): to pass under a wave by rolling the board over.
Wave hog: someone that gets more waves than you.
Wax: tacky substance applied to the deck of a surfboard for traction.
Weak: a wave (or a surfing move) that has little power. E.g., the swell is weak, or that guy's turn was weak.
Wedge: a peaky wave formed by refraction from the shore. E.g., *The Wedge*, is the name of a break that rebounds of off a jetty in Newport Beach, California.
Whitewater: the foam of a breaking wave.
Width: the dimension of a surfboard at its widest spot across the deck, perpendicular to the stringer.
Wind swell: short period swell caused by local winds.
Wind wave: a wave generated by wind swell.
Wipeout: to involuntarily fall while surfing.
Wrap: a bend in the swell or breaking wave as it turns to follow the shoreline.

www.ingramcontent.com/pod-product-compliance
Lightning Source LLC
Chambersburg PA
CBHW051953290426
44110CB00015B/2225